Table of Contents

Part Three: The Kid

Part Four: Last Act of the Pre-9/11 Era

Dedication

For my son, my students and Adele

Acknowledgments

To Anna Pinger for her painstaking work and computer wizardry.

Introduction

In the profile of William Hickey in this book, the actor says, "Art is the opposite of life. In life, we never know the end. In art, we know the end but never the beginning."

To reduce such vagueness here, some articles are preceded by explanations of how they came about. After all, although many names and identifying details have been changed, in the end, the purpose of writing is to reveal; life is mysterious enough. (This is not to say that even the autobiographical articles adhere strictly to the rules of nonfiction. They partake of a genre somewhere on the spectrum between "gonzo journalism" and "based on a true story.")

A word about those people whose identities have been changed: There's still a lingering sense of guilt about them, no matter how thoroughly their tracks have been covered. One is always describing their most unattractive traits, their most insensitive moments. Writing isn't a nice profession – you end up biting the hand that feeds you. The English teacher described in Writer Wannabe Seeks Brush with Death, for instance, comes off as uncaring to the point of callousness. She was the opposite but as an adolescent, I managed to play the role of victim whenever the opportunity presented itself. It's partly because of her that I write at all.

Part One:

Musicians

To Everything There Is a Season

The story below is based on the piano teacher I had in high school. Ten years later, while on a fellowship at Juilliard, I spoke of her to Dorothy Delay, the legendary violin teacher who said, "I'd like to meet her."

Our appointment took place at Miss Delay's studio during a lesson she was giving Nadja Salerno-Sonnenberg who, at seventeen, was already reknowned in musical circles. Normally, Nadja didn't like outsiders sitting in on her lessons (who would?) but for some reason, that day she made an exception.

"Miss Laudon" was bowled over, rising from her seat after each piece and exclaiming, "But this is simply wonderful!" I was embarrassed: Did Miss Delay regret having allowed us into the inner sanctum of her studio or was she grateful for the appreciation? Nadja was her usual blasée, modest self.

In the city, a man and a woman ran a music school. The man handled the school's business affairs and the woman gave piano lessons. The woman, Miss Laudon, taught Art and Truth in her lessons and the man, Mr. Eschenbach, gave her the most promising students.

The school was on the edge of a run-down neighborhood. One afternoon just after his fourteenth birthday, Michael Krasner passed it on his way home from the center where he earned community service credit for high school.

"Guit r Piano Ac ordi n Lan uages 10 cents," read the sign in pink neon lights with letters missing. A repeated "C" sounded through the window as an eight-year-old boy practiced his scales without ever reaching the top. But from an inner room came other music: mournful harmonies that aroused in Michael a fierce desire.

He'd taken piano lessons for four years from a woman who came to the house on Thursday after her day job at a bank. She had red fingernails that curved like a toucan's beak and she assigned him pieces – a Clementi Sonatina, a movement by Kuhnau, – that inspired no particular emotion. When Michael stopped taking lessons, she didn't seem to care.

But hearing the music now that sounded like muffled crying behind the wall, he wanted to play it the way he wanted to pitch for his school team, the Falcons. Who was playing like that? She – (Michael imagined the student to be a pale, ethereal girl,) – must be some sort of prodigy!

Michael was a shy boy but he opened the door of the school and climbed the rickety stairs to the office.

"May I help you?" bellowed Mr. Eschenbach, for he was hard of hearing. He was about seventy, with suspenders over a short-sleeved shirt and a lopsided bow tie. He reminded Michael of Pinocchio's maker, Geppetto.

"I'd, um, like some information about piano lessons?" said Michael.

"Piano! Sure, we got piano! We got the best teacher in New York – Miss Laudon. She's the best – " he searched for a suitable place – "anywhere!" He spoke in clichés because English was new to him and the clichés seemed fresh. "You wait here. She'll be finished, five minutes. Sit over there." Michael sat where Mr. Eschenbach waved.

"You're a nice boy. I can tell," Mr. Eschenbach went on approvingly while they waited. "Nice manners... Don't worry. You came to the right place."

Michael squirmed nervously as he tried not to giggle at the old man's insistence.

"What's the matter, you don't believe me?"

Michael assured Mr. Eschenbach he believed him.

"I tell you something," Mr. Eschenbach confided. "Miss Laudon's not just a great musician and a great teacher..." His eyes widened as though he were describing an apparition. "She's a great human being!"

The romantic harmonies from the inner room stopped and a young woman came out. She didn't look the way Michael had imagined, slender and beautiful. She was small and dumpy.

"Bye," she whispered to Mr. Eschenbach as though imparting a secret.

"Bye, Sweetie. See you Saturday," Mr. Eschenbach called. "Wait here," he told Michael. "She'll be right out." And he went to get Miss Laudon.

A minute or so later, Michael heard arguing around the corner at the end of the hall.

"No, no," a woman complained. "That's Tuesday, don't you remember? Arnold's Monday."

"Arnold's Monday?" That was Mr. Eschenbach's voice. "What happened to Thursday?"

"Aach. I'll show you later. Where's the new boy?"

A woman in her sixties appeared, walking towards Michael briskly, as though on a mission. She carried herself straight so that Michael didn't realize until she reached him that she only came up to his chin.

If Mr. Eschenbach resembled a gatekeeper, Miss Laudon was chateleine of the house. She had an aura of grace which Michael felt as soon as she took his hand in both of hers.

"I'm so happy to meet you," she said and it seemed to be true. Her eyes, lively blue, looked into his. Her hair was soft and white. "What's your name?"

"Michael... Krasner."

"It's a pleasure to meet you, Michael. Come in, please."

She led him down the hall past the practice cubicles, each empty but for a lopsided piano with brown or missing teeth. When they reached her studio, Miss Laudon gestured towards the piano, the school's one grand, and shut the door.

"You've studied before?"

"Well, up until June. I had about four years but – "

"It doesn't matter. What would you like to play?"

Michael named the piece he had played at the eighth grade spring recital. "Fantasy in D Minor by Mozart."

Miss Laudon nodded. "Please – Begin."

She sat up straight, with the somber expression of one who is about to perform a religious office. As Michael played the opening, she listened like a doctor to a heartbeat. The Fantasy wasn't Michael's favorite piece, – it wasn't as exciting as Anitra's Tanz – but he was a diligent student and played as his teacher had instructed him.

"Yes, I see," said Miss Laudon, stopping him after eight bars. "Thank you." She came over to the piano.

"Please start again." Michael lifted his hand.

"Ssh...!" said Miss Laudon as he was about to play the first note. "A shadow of sound... far away..." While Michael played, she described the emerging scene.

"And now... the theme... pleading." She sang along with the piano, her voice heavy with pathos. "Da da dee da da." On the high D, Miss Laudon's voice croaked. Michael shook with suppressed laughter. But his hands shook too so he stopped laughing.

As he played the successive sections Miss Laudon frowned, waltzed or marched according to their mood. Michael was embarrassed as though she was dancing naked. He wanted the lesson to be over so he could go home and sit at the kitchen table with his mother and tell her about this crazy woman.

"So!" exclaimed Miss Laudon at the end of the lesson. "You're a lovely boy. I mean that sincerely." She seemed to be pleading with him to believe her.

Michael nodded. He did believe she meant it. The thought that he was a boy whom people might describe as "lovely" calmed him, making him feel strong and gentle.

"And musical," Miss Laudon went on with encouraging emphasis.

"So now! Would you like to study with me?" she asked, looking at him with the eagerness of a child. He could not betray her trust any more than he could lie to his mother about something important.

"Sure, I guess," he said. "I'll have to ask my Mom but she didn't want me to stop taking lessons anyway, so..."

Michael's mother agreed to the piano lessons even though the price was many times that advertised by the neon sign in the window.

The following week Miss Laudon gave Michael two pieces: A movement by Haydn that was too slow for Michael's taste and a Rhapsody by Brahms he couldn't wait to play. He worked hard on the Brahms and looked forward to showing Miss Laudon what he'd accomplished. The Haydn was a duty but he learned the section Miss Laudon had assigned. Then he went back and played his favorite part of the Brahms over and over the way he ate salted peanuts when he watched T.V.

Miss Laudon praised the Brahms and sang as he played, shaping the phrases. Michael saw that what he had brought in was a piece of clay which had still to be formed.

Then he played the Haydn.

"Oh no, darling, I'm sorry," Miss Laudon said when he finished. "You've read the notes... But you mustn't play without... thinking about each note." There were tears in her eyes as she felt for the piece he had just injured.

"You're such a thoughtful boy. I can see that, even though I haven't known you long. You think before you act. You try not to hurt people. Music is like a person too. When you care about someone, you don't just learn their name. You learn all about them."

Then she made him play it again, singing with him in her wavering, croaking voice. This time he didn't feel like laughing. He felt lost so he listened. And following her voice, he began to understand the music as one might a foreign language.

Everything Mr. Eschenbach had said about Miss Laudon was true. Music was her blood, informing every gesture, moving her so as to waive the need for discipline, that mechanical substitute for love. From music came her happiness for although she got impatient with Mr. Eschenbach's forgetfulness, she was never in a bad mood.

All winter Michael worked on the two pieces Miss Laudon had given him. He loved the deep, crashing bass of the Rhapsody even though he couldn't play it with the rich tone of Arnold Gross, a boy who'd just gotten a scholarship to Juilliard. But Miss Laudon said he played "like an artist." And he loved the Haydn, now, too. When he rolled the chords, the sound filled the room like a spirit.

The competition in Michael's high school was ferocious and he did not stand out. His inconspicuousness depressed him and his depression made him even more inconspicuous. The teachers and girls he wanted to impress seemed unaware of him and he spent many hours each day devising ways to win their attention. Miss Laudon's praise gave him hope. Since he already had her attention, he did not spend hours devising ways to get it. Therefore he did not think he loved her. But she was the only person, apart from his mother, with whom he felt comfortable and happy and he was grateful for that.

It was her students, however, who captured his imagination. He wondered about them, envied them, copied their mannerisms. The dumpy woman's name was Marilyn. She was an accountant and she remained as shy as the first time he'd seen her. But when she played she was transformed, like someone saving a life. If Michael missed a lesson and had to come on Tuesday to make it up, he heard McGovern Samuels, a middle-aged man who managed a Burger King and smiled a lot. Mr. Samuels was working on Goyescas. When he played it he became serious. Expressions crossed his face as they will a dreamer's. Even though Michael had never been to Spain, he could feel the heavy, scented air and see people in the square on a summer night in Seville.

As the lessons continued, the desire that Michael had felt beneath the open window of the school the day he first passed it was fulfilled. After the Brahms and the Haydn, he learned three preludes and fugues of Bach, two Beethoven sonatas, a nocturne by Chopin and assorted pieces by Schumann and Ravel. He practiced several hours a day. On Friday when he got out of school early, he went to Lincoln Center and listened to records of symphonies and concertos, pressing the headphones to his ears to distinguish in the tinny tune of the recording the strings from the horns or clarinets. Music did not make him less sad but his sadness now expressed itself in music. When he fell in love with Gloria Rivera, a girl whose first name seemed to refer to her proportions, he heard in his mind Chopin's G Minor Ballade. If she smiled at him, his mind

15

played Beethoven's Fourth Concerto, last movement. If, as was more often the case, she ignored him, it played the Rachmaninov Second Concerto.

He also read about great musicians. The ones who were still alive – Stokowski, Boulanger, Rubinstein, – were old with long white hair. He studied their accomplished, exciting lives, and dreamed of his own following a similar path.

When Michael's upstairs neighbor complained about the practicing, he went to the music school which was open six days a week until ten.

"Take Room 8," Mr. Eschenbach would say. "Over here. Quick, before somebody comes." Or, seeing how seriously Michael was practicing, "What you were playing – Schumann? Sounds good. You work hard, maybe someday you'll grow up, play Carnegie Hall."

On Sundays, Mr. Eschenbach and Miss Laudon took a walk together. Once, Michael met them on Madison Avenue, looking in the shop windows and once in the park, where they were watching the "young people."

Never having seen them outdoors, Michael took in their appearance with heightened curiosity. Miss Laudon wore a black coat and a scarf imprinted with music in a composer's hasty hand. In venturing out of the school, Mr. Eschenbach seemed to have donned years along with his overcoat; Miss Laudon had linked her arm in his in support. Michael saw it as characteristic of Miss Laudon's graciousness to repay her friend's loyalty in this way.

Although he didn't think consciously about the odd

duo, he saw Miss Laudon as a protagonist of infinite depth in a play in which Mr. Eschenbach served as comic relief.

One Tuesday after he had been taking lessons from Miss Laudon for three years, Michael arrived to find the front door of the school locked. When he went home and couldn't reach Miss Laudon or Mr. Eschenbach, he called another teacher, Mr. Moskowitz. Mr. Moskowitz said Mr. Eschenbach had had a sudden illness. He did not know when Miss Laudon would be back but it would probably not be for a while. Michael asked if Mr. Eschenbach was in the hospital. Mr. Moskowitz hesitated before answering, "He died. Day before yesterday."

The next time Michael called Miss Laudon, a strange woman answered. She said that Miss Laudon was not available at the moment but that she had asked for Michael to come see her the following day at five o'clock, if possible.

It was an afternoon in April, evening hovering above the roofs of the brownstones, the sky already painted over the park. Cold gusts started suddenly in the warm, still air. Winter and spring mingled like currents bound in opposite directions.

Miss Laudon answered the door, her eyes pink and washed-out blue.

"Come in," she said. Michael followed her to a table on which lay papers in disarray.

"I don't know what to do with all these papers. Well, you can see for yourself what this place looks like... What do you mean, 'not too bad?' It's chaos! It looks nice, usually.

'I don't know what to do. But you understand. You're such a nice boy.

'I don't know when I'll go back to school. Everybody tells me I should start teaching as soon as I can; it's better for me. But you see how much I have to do – he died so suddenly.

'I don't know when they can open the school again. He did everything. Mr. Moskowitz came in, I know, but he didn't really do very much."

"Why doesn't Mr. Moskowitz help you with all this work?" Michael asked. "Why do you have to do everything?"

"Darling, he was my husband. You didn't know that? Nobody knew at the school, except of course, the other people who worked there, who knew us for years."

It had never occurred to Michael that Miss Laudon and Mr. Eschenbach might be married. They called each other by their last names! He continued to look at Miss Laudon without showing his surprise.

"He didn't want anybody to know. Whenever we went anywhere, he just said I was his sweetheart." Saying the word, Miss Laudon broke off her explanation to cry.

"Forty-nine years we were married. It'll be fifty in October. I can show you some pictures. They should be over here, somewhere."

She went to a smaller table where more papers lay on the photograph album. On top was a newspaper clipping.

"Here's the obituary. They put it in on Wednesday.

He died Sunday night. No, Monday. No, no, no, what am I talking about. Sunday, Sunday. He went like that. They all tell me how lucky he was. Never sick a day in his life. Then, just like that. You know, he always said when he got sick, that would be it. Here, here's what they wrote in the column. Isn't that nice?"

She showed Michael the notice sent to the Times by the school expressing their sorrow.

"Here are the pictures. This is Mr. Eschenbach and myself when we got married. I like myself in this picture; I like it very much, don't you?" Michael smiled and said he did.

"You know I always say what I believe, don't I? Here. This is my daughter Margaret. You spoke to her the other day when you called. Now I want to show you my grandson."

Michael watched in a trance like someone listening to the dénouement of a court case when the defendant breaks down and tells the whole story.

"Wait a minute. Now where's that picture? Wait just a minute. Here it is. That's my little grandson when he was, I'd say, five or six."

"What's his name?" Michael asked.

"His name is Simon. That's an unusual name. You don't find many people with that name although my daughter tells me it's more common over in... What's that country... you know, England! That's right. My daughter loves England. When she was little, she used to know all the kings and queens.

'I was talking to my daughter the other day and she said, 'You know what I miss about him? His suspenders!' Oh I know it sounds funny but it's those little things!" she cried, her eyes blurred again in anguish.

When she had spent her grief, Michael went home. He didn't see her again until September, the week before he left for college. He'd decided to major in music. He couldn't turn his back on the vision she'd shown him.

She was calmer than she'd been in the spring. She showed him pictures of her family again, then remembered that Michael had visited her when Mr. Eschenbach had died. Mr. Moskowitz had taken Mr. Eschenbach's place at the school, she said. Teachers often quit (the job paid minimum wage) and sometimes, until he found a replacement, Mr. Moskowitz asked Miss Laudon to fill in. But she wasn't as young as she used to be; not like the old days when she could work 'til eight or nine and get up the next day. Her daughter told her to complain but Miss Laudon didn't want to. Mr. Moskowitz needed her, she said.

Michael wrote her a letter from college describing his music courses. She answered in a fluently written letter, punctuated by dashes, about the death of her husband. Each sentence fragment seemed to stand for some ruin of her former world.

At college, Michael studied piano with a well-known teacher, Ernest Kroll. Mr. Kroll was a Renaissance man. In addition to music, he was knowledgeable about literature, art and wine. His walls were hung with pictures of himself laughing with Messiaen, at a rehearsal with Stockhausen, receiving an honorary degree from a college in Georgia.

But he did not love music in the primal, human way of Miss Laudon. When Michael played the Chopin Fantaisie Mr. Kroll sighed, "You know, Michael, the world runs according to Darwin's theory of the survival of the fittest." Then, referring to his star pupil, "Have you heard Donna Kim play this piece? Ask her to play it for you some time." Mr. Kroll was not able and, had he been able, would have felt it beneath him to explain to Michael in song, dance or drama, the meaning of a musical phrase or particular harmony.

Meanwhile, other subjects beckoned to Michael. The temptation to study them was one which he resisted. He felt guilty about his desire to drift from the straight and narrow path of music. For while psychology and literature nourished his brain, music still lived in his heart which he considered the superior organ. So although he got better grades in English, he felt that music was his path to enlightenment.

But fate did not agree. Perhaps Mr. Kroll was right and Michael, as one of the less fit was, as a pianist, less equipped to survive. Or perhaps what changed Michael's attitude was Malamud – when he gave a series of lectures at the college – and a handful of other writers and professors who, like Stokowski, Boulanger and Rubinstein, had accomplished, exciting lives. (All were old and many had long white hair although Malamud was bald.)

More likely it was a question of hormones; a

satisfaction and resulting ebb of desire. For as Michael grew older, music drained from him. The facility he gained in college put the music he'd always wanted to play literally at his fingertips. But it was too late. The greatest works – Beethoven, Chopin, Bach – maintained their power over him but he was no longer in love. No longer did the harmonies of Schumann play all day in his head. He left music behind as though waking from a dream. He spent his twenties in a series of unfulfilling jobs and put his energy into writing a novel. All that was left of music in his life was an ideal to strive for in his writing.

One day, Michael saw Miss Laudon on the street, looking in the shop windows as she walked home with a bag from the supermarket. She was wearing the same black coat she had had when he was a student. When Michael reached her, she was studying the components of a model bathroom with faux-brass faucets and claws on the bathtub.

"Miss Laudon?" Michael said.

"What?" She turned around and focused on his face.

"Michael!" She opened her arms and they embraced.

Beneath her coat, Miss Laudon was thinner.

"How are you?!" she exclaimed but her enthusiasm now seemed forced.

As the two talked, they scanned each other's faces for change. Miss Laudon's eyes were duller, the blue turning the color of dish water.

"Fine. How are you?"

"Oh, well, you know Mr. Eschenbach died. Yes, yes, of course, what am I talking about? You were there. You were such a lovely boy. I know you must be a fine young man. Yes, yes," she insisted over Michael's demurral. "I can tell. I have an instinct about people, you know. Did you know that? I'll bet you have it too. You can tell if someone is a... a good person, a fine person, what they call in Yiddish a 'mensch!' Do you know what that is? You do. I can tell that about you, see?

'How's your mother?" she asked, the attempted enthusiasm returning.

"Fine."

"Have you been to any concerts?"

"Not recently."

"Did you hear De Larrocha when she was here?"

"No, I didn't."

"Oh, it was something! And Bolet, did you go to hear him?"

"No."

"Beautiful concert! I was there all day for the rehearsal. He came in the afternoon around one. First he played the E Major Scherzo of Chopin, you remember – Dah dah dee dah dum..." She became hushed as she sang the opening and Michael saw that as a musician, she hadn't changed.

The conversation, which consisted of accounts of concerts Michael had missed and questions about matters he'd left behind years before, lasted forty minutes. The next time he saw Miss Laudon on the street, he pretended interest in a nearby newsstand until she passed.

Over the years that followed, Michael called Miss

Laudon twice – once when he married and again when his first child was born. She talked of artists – especially De Larrocha and Bolet – the mention of their names reawakening her enthusiasm for their playing. Michael listened with the patience of a sober guest pacifying an intoxicated one. He saw that music was her element and that her spirit was like a deer: Though unwanted in the garden of his present life, it had been beautiful in the woods of his youth.

Rosalyn Tureck

I first met Rosalyn Tureck, the pianist and Bach specialist who died in 2003, one summer when, having nothing else to do, I registered for a lecture series she was giving at the Lincoln Center Library.

It was an eye-opening experience for a sixteen-year-old. Tureck was my first Grande Dame, a species which has since vanished in this increasingly politically correct world. Her abundant brown hair was swept up in a chignon (which I would later see removed and tucked away in the closet,) and her stage-presence was imposing though in fact, she was tiny – even when she wore high heels, she walked on tiptoe. (Once, after I'd known her several years, she answered the door in a towel and tiptoed, barefoot, back to the shower.)

The audience consisted of college students, piano teachers thirsting for knowledge from the fountainhead, retirees and aesthetes who believed Bach should only be played on the harpsichord. Tureck made short work of the last group, showing that Bach's music is abstract: He transcribed freely from one instrument to another, depending on what was on hand.

There were lectures on ornamentation which Tureck transformed into an art in itself; the kinship between Bach and Chinese music; the distorting influence of the Romantic era on Bach; Bach and twentieth century music. (Tureck had made her Carnegie Hall debut at the age of seventeen playing not a keyboard but a new electronic instrument

– the Theremin – which is most often heard these days in movies when a ghostly atmosphere is called for.) Yet she was far from being a "purist:" "The purists believe that to reveal emotion in Bach is like a lady letting her slip show," she said.

Much of her work consisted of undoing the stereotypical attitudes people have towards Bach. In one master class, for instance, a middle-aged piano teacher who was playing the Prelude to the B Flat Partita changed the ornament when the subject entered in the middle of the piece.

"Why did you do that?" Tureck asked.

"I don't know; instinct," the woman replied.

"Instinct," Tureck repeated with the hollow laugh of one who has heard the response a thousand times. "What you call 'instinct' comes from a tradition of the nineteenth century that you've been hearing your whole life. Bach doesn't change ornaments within a subject. Tell me, did you do it for 'variety?'"

The quotation marks curled sarcastically around the word with what writers used to call "thinly veiled contempt."

"Yes."

Tureck nodded. Where to begin? Bach does not need us to spice up his work and it degrades him even to explain that.

"Trust Bach," she said. "He knew what he was doing."

(Five years later when I was studying with her in

Oxford, she played an ornament inconsistently; I asked her why.

"For asymmetry."

I looked at her suspiciously: "I thought you didn't approve of doing things for variety."

She laughed that knowing, seductive chuckle that made her sound like Carmen beckoning from a doorway.

"I think it's a distinction *with* a difference.")

One night as she was talking about ornamentation in Chinese music, a theme I'd heard her expound on before, my mind wandered: There was Mary C. in the previous night's master class who had played the E Minor Partita so intensely. What wouldn't I give?...

Then a phrase drifted by that jolted me awake:

"...I've known this since my revelation when I was seventeen."

What was that?

"...A revelation I had while playing one of the fugues from the Well-Tempered Clavier."

For God's sake, tell us about your revelation! To hell with everything else.

At the end of the lecture she announced: "Thursday evening is our last for this session. I will accept questions from the audience. These should be written down and given to one of the ushers during intermission and I will devote the final hour to addressing a few of them."

The next day I took out her recording of the Well-Tempered Clavier, both books, and listened to the whole thing, searching for the fugue that had inspired her revelation. Her playing of the Fugue in A Minor, Book I, was determined as though to prove something. I thought, "This is it."

Thursday night, come intermission, I wrote out my question and gave it to the usher who was collecting scraps of paper from members of the audience.

The final hour arrived. Tureck answered questions on ornamentation. Then she said: "The last question is about me." She looked at the slip of paper I'd handed in and read: "In your revelation when you were seventeen, what was revealed to you?"

She smiled intimately as though we'd settled in front of the fire for a tête-à-tête.

"It was a Wednesday in December, a few days after my 17th birthday. I was playing the A Minor Fugue from Book One of the Well-Tempered Clavier. And I realized how I must play Bach from now on. I fainted. When I woke up, I worked in this new way that had been *shown* to me, really.

'That week, instead of bringing in my usual three Preludes and Fugues to Mme. Samaroff, I brought in only one. I explained to Mme. Samaroff what had happened and how I was going to approach Bach from now on. She said, 'You'll never be able to do it.'"

Tureck smiled for the moral, of course, was, "But as you see, the rest is history."

That was it. Tantalizing stuff. But she hadn't said what had been revealed to her.

After the lecture I went back and stood on line in the

"green room" to pay homage. All concert halls have green rooms though few of them are green.

"Are you a pianist?" she asked.

I mumbled something appropriately modest.

She took my right hand and stretched apart the third and fourth fingers.

"With hands like that, you shouldn't give up."

The gypsy had spoken. It made my summer. In those days, I had faith in experts.

Five years later, while I was studying at Oxford, Tureck gave some lectures there. Isaiah Berlin had helped secure her a Fellowship and an honorary doctorate and she had an unaccustomed amount of free time on her hands.

Because of Oxford's low-key approach to publicity, the first lecture was delivered to an audience of two. One was a man who would have left except that he didn't want to be conspicuous; the other was me.

Ever the pro, Tureck went through the lecture with as much enthusiasm as though the house had been packed. I've liked to tell myself that my rapt attention in part made up for the lack of numbers.

Knowing my admiration for Tureck, my Music History tutor arranged for me to have five lessons with her.

She was a generous teacher who didn't count the clock but continued the lesson for two hours or however long it took to say what she had to say. She didn't count her payment either; the college was offering her a nominal sum. (However a salesman at Steinway once told me, with an edge, "She certainly is a good businesswoman.")

After the lessons, we went to Evensong. Although the service at Christ Church is more reknowned, Tureck, a Bach specialist rather than a splashy showwoman, preferred the intimate setting of the chapel at Magdalen. However, she refrained from the standing and kneeling that were part of the ritual for believers.

She also got a kick out of the Oxford Boat Races and a lunch she'd been invited to at an eighteenth-century house by the side of a stream.

"So recherché," she said with the sort of nostalgia one feels for a past one never had.

She was ahead of her time in every arena. The contents of her book shelves ranged from science – particularly topology, in which she saw a kinship to Bach – to Joyce and Burgess who had experimented with fugue as a literary form, to The Joy of Sex. Her kitchen cabinets were stocked with organic food decades before the practise, which I believe she'd been introduced to by Yehudi Menuhin, became fashionable.

Everything about her was grand, even her pettiness. She didn't bother to put down ordinary people – she saved her bitchiness for Glenn Gould and then she let it rip. When he died at fifty of a cerebral hemorrhage she said, "Not surprising, considering how tightly he played." Guiltily, I thought she had a point although I also thought she might have exercised some hypocrisy and let his dust settle before saying so.

The people she esteemed were composers and scientists. They were the creative ones in whose presence she became humble. (One of her several husbands was a scientist who died two years after the wedding. "That marriage would have lasted," she said. Another marriage had ended within a few days. An obituary in the Guardian states that she was married only once, at the age of fifty, to George Wallingford Downs, an architect who died the same year. [1]) Great as her talent was, she regretted it did not extend into the realm of composition although her approach to ornamentation and improvisation in Bach certainly bordered on that art.

What was most inspiring about her was her absolute confidence. Whether it was real or a defense I don't know or care. (In truth, it was probably fragile. Rumor has it that she had a nervous breakdown in her twenties, putting her head down on her arm in the middle of a concert – which she herself was giving – and going to sleep.) It's what enabled her to make a career out of Bach which had never been done before and probably never will be again. It's why she could play the Goldberg Variations on the piano which of course has only one keyboard rather than the harpsichord which has two: "No one had told me it was impossible." She was fond of quoting the American astronauts: "Difficult things take a while; the impossible, a little longer."

She spoke of playing in India for Indira Gandhi after which she joined the invited audience for dinner. The hall was so vast, she said, that the two hundred guests looked like a cozy dinner party. For dessert, they were served cake with gold icing.

Back at the college dorm, I consulted my Indian neighbor about this.

"Gold!" she scoffed. "Nobody eats gold. Now silver, yes, we eat."

One night with George, a graduate student in Music History whom I was dating, I invited Tureck to dinner. George ordered fish which he had a hard time filleting.

"Pass that over here," Tureck said. "You have to know about anatomy for this." She was being arch as she proceeded deftly to guide the knife through the fish, thereby revealing its feathery bones. "One day you'll be able to tell people about the night Tureck showed you how to dissect a fish."

I thought, "How she must despise us, to think that we will look back on this as one of the high points of our lives. So why is she spending the evening with us?"

We talked about what a small world Oxford was. I told the story of a letter I'd received in spite of a comically bungled address (garbled name, wrong college.)

"That's nothing," Tureck said. "I used to get letters addressed to Rosalyn Tureck, London, England."

She seemed to hover on the verge of delusions of grandeur – (once when I answered the phone in New York she said, "This is Madame,") – until one remembered that the boasted accomplishments were real.

"What is your thesis about?" she asked George.

"German lieder of the post-Romantic era."

"Mmm... How decadent," she said suggestively. "And are you a composer yourself?"

"I wouldn't call myself a composer though I've written a few songs. To poetry of that period, as a matter of fact."

"Hm! You must play them for me some time. Have they been performed?"

"Yes. A student at the Royal College performed them for her jury last year. As her twentieth century piece."

"Really!"

The flattering two-way banter went on as I grew angrier at being ignored, used as a catalyst for this marriage of two kindred spirits. She seemed to think she already knew my type so she didn't need to ask me anything.

"We should order dessert," I said. "They're closing in fifteen minutes and the waiter's giving us dirty looks."

"Well!" Tureck said with amused astonishment at the vigor of my annoyance. (*There's life in the little nebish yet.*)

"Let's ask for the menu, then, shall we?"

"About your revelation when you were seventeen," I said, my boldness feeding on the point I'd just scored. "What was revealed to you?"

She laughed and took a deep breath. "Play the long notes long and the short notes short."

By this time I knew her well enough to understand this gnomic, if seemingly banal, statement. (When I told this story to a music critic years later, he scoffed as at an instance of "in vino veritas.")

What she meant was this: The written score is only a potential thing. The performer "realizes" it in the sense of making it real. Her job corresponds to that of the creator in

33

that she must reveal what he has conceived. She must not add, but simply make real.

After Oxford closed for the summer, Tureck invited me to go apartment hunting with her in London.

First we stopped at the bank where she fumbled with her checkbook before giving up in frustration saying, with a dismissive wave, "You do this."

I was surprised to find someone who knew less about coping in the world than I did.

Atop the London bus we rode out to St. Johns' Wood, marveling over the G Flat chord in the Chromatic Fantasy in D Minor. A G Flat chord in that key is, in Bach's time as in any other, virtually unheard of. (The apartment, she decided, was "too quiet.")

I left Oxford at the same time as Tureck and moved to the same neighborhood in New York where we occasionally got together. She was looking for an assistant, a lady-in-waiting, really, and asked if I'd like the job.

What she had in mind, I knew, was a factotum: Secretary, maid, slave, shrink...

I was busy, I said.

But I had a small repertoire of dishes I could cook and I wanted to make one for her: A cheese omelette. The secret lay in adding milk to the eggs before whipping them up. Pesto was good too, mixed in with the eggs.

One night, a week before a concert Tureck was to give in Carnegie Hall, I went over to make her such an omelette for dinner. Again she brought up the subject of my working for her. I didn't say anything. But in retrospect it's clear that she took my silence to mean that at least for that one night, I was her employee.

"Actually, I don't feel in the mood for eggs tonight," she said as I got down to work. "Steak, I think, very lean. Go down to the butcher on sixty-seventh, this side of the street. Not the one on sixty-sixth." Her voice grew imperious. "And don't be longer than twenty minutes!" And she slammed the door.

I thought about calling it quits on the whole evening. But I didn't want to back out of a commitment.

After dinner she asked again if I knew anyone who might want to be her assistant.

"Someone with intelligence, sensitivity..."

"You mean, to be a secretary?"

"Not just that." She waxed lyrical. "It's a job that requires subtlety, ingenuity."

I mentally added, "And a dose of masochism."

"You mean, like a maid?"

"Yes," she conceded. She looked at me suggestively.

"Sorry, I don't know anybody."

"Perhaps one of your parents' friends," she said disdainfully.

Then I stooped to a defense tactic of last resort: Name-dropping. "Well, Peter Sellers is dead," I said with a bitchery equal to hers – or so I thought.

Without missing a beat, she waved aside the sarcastic suggestion.

"He wouldn't have been suitable anyway," she replied with what was either impressive quick-wittedness or insanity.

"Go get my checkbook from the desk in the living-room." (She was sitting up in bed.)

"I didn't do this for money."

"Well then," she said, becoming coy, "would you take a ticket to the concert?"

"I'd love one."

"Call my secretary tomorrow and have her put aside ONE ticket. What do I owe you for the meat?"

"Four seventy-two."

She ripped out a check and signed it. "Here," she said, handing me the blank check. "Fill in the amount."

When I got the ticket for the concert I noted the price: fifteen dollars, exactly what I would have earned had I accepted the standard rate at that time of a maid for the three hours I'd been there.

One night about eight years later and after my son Alex (not his real name) was born, I ran into Tureck on the street. She was with the feminist writer, Marilyn French, whom she was taking for dinner at her club. Afterwards, I read a book by French in which a character says that all men are rapists at heart. The character is killed.

The assessment of men stuck with me until I wrote to French asking, among other things, if she had a son.

Yes, she answered, and reproached me for a common mistake among readers: That of assuming that a character is a spokesperson for the writer. The character's view was untenable, French said, which was why she had died.

When I saw Tureck again, we spoke of French's book. I mentioned the character who believed that all men have the instinct for rape.

"Do you believe that?" Tureck asked.

"I can't afford to, can I?" I said, alluding to my son.

"No," she smiled.

The last time I saw her, I brought Alex, then two, to her apartment which was stuffed with rare old instruments and artifacts from grateful fans all over the world. To keep Alex occupied, on the way over I bought a piece of poundcake from the deli. He crumbled it happily for half an hour. But crumbs and ants were a small price to pay to keep the instruments intact. Tureck thought he was adorable. She then returned to Oxford for the next thirteen years or so.

A few years ago, my friend Miriam showed me an article in which Tureck had been quoted. A cantor at her temple had been accused of molesting a young boy and Tureck, as a well-known congregant, was asked her opinion.

"It's terrible if true," she said.

It took a while before I acted on the information that she was in town. I was working with a coalition of scientists, parents and Lower Manhattan residents, trying to get the EPA to do a proper cleanup around Ground Zero.

Alex, now seventeen, had been a student at Stuyvesant High School, four blocks north of the World Trade Center, on 9/11. Life was fraught so that I could never think about anything else until Friday evening which is not a great time to be calling a temple for contact info. But eventually I got her number.

A housekeeper answered the phone. Tureck was playing the piano as robustly as ever in the background.

She was living in Riverdale, with a view of endless sky, she said. A friend, a conductor who'd been her student when he was twelve, had recommended the place. He and his wife lived nearby.

"I came home to end my days," Tureck said, with more equanimity than I would have expected her to show in the face of death. I later wished I'd understood how literally she was speaking.

She was writing her autobiography which would have thirty chapters.

"One for each variation," I said, alluding to the Goldberg Variations.

"Very good," she said.

I told her about the work we were doing at Ground Zero. She was intrigued. But as the country was about to go to war with Iraq, her more pressing questions were about that. Were there petitions to squelch the idea as she'd like to sign and maybe make some phone-calls?

Yes, lots, I said, and sent them to her, along with Hillary Clinton's fax number and other contact info. I also sent her a poem I'd written about 9/11 which appears at the end of this book. I wondered what she'd make of the quatrain:

WTC, those letters,
Now a code for grief and fear...
When I was studying music they
Stood for the Well-Tempered Clavier.

She said that in the spring I should come up and visit.

Spring came – along with the Iraq war – and went, as the war did not. The battle of Ground Zero also continued with no end in sight. When I saw that Tureck had died, I reproached myself for not having called to see if she wanted to make good on the invitation to visit. Then I reflected that burying myself in work is what she would have done. But the rationale rang hollow and I regretted having let the time slip by.

As I read her obituary I thought, "She was one of a kind," but no, she wasn't. For what "kind" would that be? She taught me important lessons about many things besides Bach. They constitute the revelation that began the summer I was sixteen.

Addendum: *In 2005, the Juilliard bulletin reported that Albert Glinsky, a graduate, had published a biography entitled Theremin: Ether Music and Espionage. Apparently the Russian-born composer had had an interest in the eponymous instrument he invented which was not solely musical; it could also be used to spy for his country.*

What did Tureck, whose grandfather had been a leading cantor in Kiev, know of this? She had certainly rubbed elbows with some well-known spooks: Isaiah Berlin, for instance, who had helped secure her honorary doctorate from, and position at, Oxford.[2]

But even if someone had asked this when she was alive, she couldn't have given a straight answer anyway.

Nadia Boulanger

The last summer that Nadia Boulanger, the legendary musical pedagogue, taught at Fontainebleau, I went to study choral conducting with her. Starting with Aaron Copland, generations of American musicians had made the pilgrimage there or to Paris (her winter residence) where, in between lessons, Boulanger acted as guru to Stravinsky, Bernstein and virtually every composer who had dabbled in neoclassicism. Yet despite her Who's Who list of protégées, she wasn't particular about choosing students. Anyone could go; you'd just be placed in classes according to your ability. So a séjour with Boulanger became a necessary rite of passage for any music student who'd heard tell of her, usually from one who'd gone before. And of these there were many. The composer and critic Virgil Thompson once observed, "Every town in America has a church, a firehouse and a pupil of Nadia Boulanger."

The following account is drawn from memory with the exception of the names of students or details of dialogue which have been filled in by imagination.

Because of illness she missed the first class of the session. We wondered if this was it: Was she finally taking to her bed for good? But as was her custom, she rallied in time for the second class.

So on a Wednesday afternoon in July, right after lunch, forty of us sat in an airy room of the Fontainebleau château (loaned for the purpose by the French government who had taken a notoriously long time to recognize their exalted citizen), excitedly awaiting our audience with the woman I thought of as the most influential teacher since Mohammed. (Ned Rorem once called her, "the most influential teacher since Socrates."[3])

Most of us were students of her disciples so we knew the legends which pointed to an asceticism and single-mindedness we could barely grasp:

1. As a girl, she had kept herself awake one night out of three to memorize the entire canon of Western music starting with Gregorian chant. By all accounts, she succeeded.

2. For twenty years, she performed in the same black dress. Finally Princess Grace, who had given it to her, said, "Don't you think it's time for a new dress?" "Yes," replied Boulanger. "Get me another exactly the same."

3. A journalist asked her how it felt to be the first woman to conduct the New York Philharmonic. "I have been a woman for fifty years," Boulanger replied, "and long since overcome my initial astonishment."

4. An aide told her she'd been invited to receive an award by Valéry Giscard d'Estaing, then President of France. "Who is that?" she asked.

5. After a dinner party at the home of Princess Grace, she reported, "I sat next to the most interesting man. He knew Shakespeare by heart and spoke it

so beautifully... But I understand he has had a very scandalous life."

The man was Richard Burton, then party to the most famous divorce case of the decade.

After we'd been waiting on the edge of our literal seats for fifteen minutes, Boulanger was wheeled in. Blind, unaware she'd arrived, she was lurched over to the left. True to form, she was dressed in black. Her hands lay in her lap, too large for it now that the rest of her had shriveled. Gnarled and inert, they were nonetheless recognizable from the photographs we'd seen of Boulanger in her fifties pointing out to Stravinsky some passage in a fresh score. The plain nails were those of hard-working hands; a religious, perhaps.

In the first row, Louise Talma, the head of the Music Department at Hunter College, watched the progress of the wheelchair down the aisle with a fixed stare as though to communicate to the body within it her will to get it through the hour. A Boulanger student fifty years earlier, she'd become the first woman composer admitted to the National Academy of Arts and Letters and had been sought after as a collaborator by Thornton Wilder, making her the envy of her contemporaries among American composers. Since her student days, she'd returned to Fontainebleau every two years to consult with Boulanger on her latest commission.

She wore a light grey suit in the style of a younger Boulanger; "Mademoiselle's" acolytes tended to acquire her habits in both the quotidian and the religious senses of that word. Talma's hair was a variant of Boulanger's chignon and her eyes, like Boulanger's in years past, expressed nothing beyond a fervent (some might have said "fanatical") discipline. Her other features, like her room back at the hotel, gave no clue into character. They were simply there to function as she had been put on this earth to work. Her sturdy hands, a peasant's, were folded in her lap.

At the entrance of the god of Musical Pedagogy, silence fell.

For Boulanger was a god to us. In the beginning was the Word but before the Word was the Sound whose mysteries she was closer to understanding than anyone alive. A pupil of Fauré at the age of eight, she was our link to d'Indy; through him, to Rameau whose treatise on Harmony was the foundation of the principles of all Western music.

Strictly speaking, Boulanger didn't think of herself as God but she did have an unusually close relationship to Him. She went to Mass every day and into mourning annually for a week at the anniversary of the death of her sister, Lili, who had succumbed to TB at the age of twenty-four. And as often happens with nonagenarians, the people of whom she spoke most affectionately – Bach, Beethoven, Stravinsky – were all dead.

Humble in the face of the Absolute, she could be ruthless to those of lesser stuff. While the histrionics of some of the Juilliard faculty were reknowned, Boulanger expressed her disapproval in coldness which, unlike heat, can attain to an absolute degree. She adhered to an idiosyncratic variant of the well-known French adage: *I think; therefore, I am*. Her version went: "I think, therefore it is." Stories abounded of how she'd turned her back on an old student because he or she had experimented with electronic music. She also partook of the prejudices of her era which included favoring men. Upon mastering a difficult exercise, a student called Greta Simms found herself promoted to the rank of "Monsieur Seem."

According to rumor, a student had once complained at the end of her lesson that she didn't feel well.

"You must overcome the weakness of the flesh," Boulanger replied and sent the student home.

It was raining and the student died of pneumonia. Thereafter Boulanger always inquired anxiously about the health of her students.

Mlle. A., secretary, long-time companion and now guide of the wheelchair, leaned over and whispered that they'd arrived in the classroom. She was a frayed, distracted woman with strands of wiry hair that was losing its color along with its form as it escaped numerous bobby pins. She wore beige socks and a skirt and blouse that looked as though she'd picked them up at a jumble sale.

When she crossed the palace courtyard, she hugged the wall like a nun in her cloister, holding her sweater close regardless of the heat. She smiled uncertainly at students; if one addressed her, she shrank back, startled.

Boulanger's hands moved slowly like a medium's in her lap, the right, attempting to rise and giving up. Her speech was also slow and hesitant, with a quality of the

Beyond.

"Thank you for coming such a long way, from so many different countries. I hope you will work very hard and learn many things.

'Mlle. Dieudonné, to whom I am most grateful, has told me you are good musicians. Is Mr. Engel, Engelho –'"

"Engelhart," Mlle. Dieudonné articulated, leaning towards the wheelchair.

"Engelhart. Is Mr. Engelhart here, please?"

Mlle. Dieudonné looked into the audience with the unblinking eyes of a bird. Small and stooped, she wore a grey shawl which, by concealing her arms, added to the avian effect. Like the old woman who lived in a shoe, she had so many students, she did not know what to do, especially since Boulanger's decline. Her teaching load had doubled and following in Boulanger's footsteps, she often taught 'til eleven o'clock at night. Dieudonné was in her eighties.

"Mr. Engelhart? Come, please," she goaded a dark, eager-eyed boy who was making his way out of the third row.

"Le voici, Mademoiselle," she said, as Arthur Engelhart sat at the piano. (*"Here he is."*)

"Can you tell me, Mr. Engelhart, how many notes are there?"

"You mean in an octave, Mademoiselle? Twelve."

"No, that is not it."

"Well I'm not sure I understand what you want – an infinite number?"

45

"No, no, no."

"Well there are eighty-eight keys on the keyboard."

"No," groaned Boulanger. It was hard to be intimidated by such a spectacle but Arthur did want to allay the old woman's frustration.

The other students turned to each other pantomiming incomprehension across the room with shrugs and open, empty hands. Somebody suggested loudly enough for the audience to hear that they could use a calculator to figure out all the notes written since Gregorian chant. A chubby girl curbed her giggles, the effort turning her pink as a ham.

"Somebody else! Bring. Me. Some. Body. Else."

Mlle. Dieudonné, who had begun to doze, awoke, startled, and froze like a squirrel who senses he is being watched. Then, like an animal who lives in a constant state of emergency she acted, grabbing Joseph Kaufman in the first row with a strength that, he later said, amazed him.

Joseph was distinguished from the rest of the student body – a body whose scruffiness was typical of undergraduates who've been away from home for two weeks in high summer – by his suit which he wore out of respect for Boulanger, although his fellow students often reminded him that she wouldn't be able to see it.

As he sat down, a hand rose from the medium's lap and reached shakily for the keyboard. Hitting two adjacent notes simultaneously it fumbled, then rose again to descend onto a note a fourth below. The spirit having tapped out its message, the hand withdrew to come to rest once more in Boulanger's lap.

"Mr. Kau –, Mr. K –, do you know how many notes there are?"

"Well, Mademoiselle, I, too, thought an infinite number."

"No," Boulanger moaned. Mlle. A. soothed her and turned the wheelchair to take it back to the apartment. Boulanger did not protest or perhaps even notice.

As soon as she rounded the corner, pandemonium broke out in the classroom.

"Mr. Kuh –, Mr. Kuh –" croaked one boy in imitation of the scene that had just taken place. Another boy did a grotesque parody of a monster drawling incoherent, preposterous demands. Mlle. Dieudonné played a thundering chord to bring us back to reality and spent the rest of the period on a tortuous musical dictation which sobered us up in no time.

The following week, Boulanger held the class for conductors in her apartment. In the interim, Emile Naoumoff, her latest protégée who had been allowed out of his native Bulgaria to study with her when he was eight, told us the answer to the question: "How many notes are there?" There are seven, all other notes being variants of the original scale. Sixteen that summer, Emile served as de facto teacher to the rest of us who were mostly in our twenties. Boulanger had once observed that he could perform musical feats that had stumped Stravinsky.

We were a group of nine, waiting outside the palace with the excitement of young people going for the first time to see the Old Country about which they've heard stories all their lives. Our ardor had not been allayed by the sorry spectacle of our first class with Boulanger. As some line in some movie pithily has it, we knew who she was.

Mlle. A. lowered the palace key in a basket from the second floor window. We let ourselves in and went upstairs where she led us into the living-room.

It was 4 P.M. and the high-ceilinged room, with long windows that looked onto the palace garden, was already steeped in shadow. My memory, into whose gaps cliché has flowed, has furnished it with tables and walls that are cluttered with pictures of friends from another era; even older pictures of family. Signed "With Admiration" or "Affectionately" were intense publicity shots of pianists; conductors in an ecstatic swirl of hair; photos of Boulanger receiving an honorary doctorate or being received by de Gaulle.

These served as reminders that thirty years before, Boulanger had been a woman of the world as well as of the Spirit. When a student became too nerdy, losing herself in music, Boulanger would provide an antidote: an invitation to a tea at which would be Bernstein with his librettist or lover; or writers whose names the student knew only from newspaper accounts to which she now wished she'd paid more attention. The conductor Andrew Litton once said that when, at the age of thirteen, he played the piano for Boulanger, she asked him to recite any poetry he knew. He couldn't and understood that he should broaden his cultural horizons. When he told this story I thought, "I would have asked you to climb a tree or throw a ball."

Boulanger sat in her wheelchair looking other-worldly, as the blind sometimes do. Mlle. Dieudonné leaned over and whispered that we'd arrived.

"Good afternoon," Boulanger said. "We will begin by conducting in 4/4 time. I will give you the tempo: Bah, bah, bah, bah."

She intoned a moderate tempo, conducting. We followed her lead.

"You must not vary the tempo no matter what else happens," she went on, conducting steadily as though the beat were a pendulum which, having been set in motion, would continue, unchanging, forever.

Her own hand returned to her lap as we continued conducting.

"For next time you will study the first three exercises of Hindemith. We will also study Bach Cantata Number 4. What beat are you on?"

"Two," someone replied.

"No! That was three! You are slowing down!"

She gave us other exercises which were designed to cultivate independence of the various compartments of the mind: dividing a beat into 3, 5, 7 or 11 equal parts doing one beat with one hand, another with the other and still others with each foot. We aspired to have the right hand not know what the left was doing. They were tasks essential for a conductor and any good musician but felt more like disciplines demanded of the Buddhist priesthood.

The next class we had with Boulanger came three weeks later by which time she had markedly declined.

Mlle. Dieudonné led us into the bedroom where Boulanger lay in a pink satin bed-jacket on a cloud of lacy pillows.

"Les élèves sont arrivés," Mlle. Dieudonné said, bending towards Boulanger's ear. (*"The pupils have arrived."*)

Mlle. A. approached from the corner to adjust the pillows. Boulanger's hand moved in the outline of a fruitless attempt to raise herself.

"I am honored to make your acquaintance," she said. "Do you play piano?"

We looked at each other in confusion. Did she think she was addressing only one person? Several of the students were primarily conductors; others played violin or cello; one played French horn; one sang. I was the only one whose first instrument was piano. The third member of Boulanger's entourage, Louise Talma, pushed me forward.

"Yes," I said.

"Play the first Prelude of Bach."

"Do you mean the C Major from the Well-Tempered Klavier?"

"Yes."

I'd never studied the piece but it is well-known and harmonically simple. Also Emile gestured that he'd come with me and whisper any chord I might not remember.

Ms. Talma frowned disapprovingly at this conspiracy but decided against waging a pantomime battle.

"Well? Why don't you begin?"

Her hand rose shakily from the sheet and waved in the air.

Taking it gently, Miss Talma returned the hand to Boulanger's side. "Le piano est dans l'autre chambre," she said softly. (*"The piano is in the other room."*)

"Ah!" At the realization of where she was, Boulanger sank further into the pillows.

I went into the living-room and began to play.

"You are not in key! Start over."

I began again.

"No!"

I looked at Mlle. Dieudonné who had posted herself in the doorway to act as mediator.

"B Flat!"

Mlle. Dieudonné shrugged and sighed. There is no B Flat in the beginning of this piece.

"Play B Flat."

I played the note.

"No, B Flat. Play B Flat."

I played the same note an octave below.

"Ah, but I see you do not know which note is B Flat. 'Annette!"

Mlle. Dieudonné returned with a resigned sigh to Boulanger's bedside like a motorized doll that goes back and forth between walls, retracing its path until someone turns it off or the motor runs out, whichever comes first.

Louise Talma looked dismayed: Boulanger had lost her perfect pitch. There followed an anxious conference of whispers.

"Play any fugue you would like."

I played the Fugue from Bach's E Minor Toccata

and, at a signal from Mlle. Dieudonné, returned to the bedroom.

"Thank you."

She had no voice left – not even a whisper; only air shaped into words which died as they left her lips. We listened in polite silence dominated by the embarrassment one feels in a courtroom for a witness who has been unmasked, her puny, shivering self revealed.

"I am sorry for this pathetic scene. A tragi-comedy."

She had been blind for several years but this seemed only to intensify her vision of the unseen. Like a star whose light won't reach us for millennia, she spoke not to the people we were then but to the people we would become over the course of a lifetime.

"You are all good musicians. I hope you will work hard. For Miss Talma and Mlle. Dieudonné."

We hung our heads and looked at the floor. For now the embarrassment was for ourselves.

Letter to Louise Talma (Never Sent)

Dear L.T.,

I've now known you over half my life. Of course,
it's impossible to know such a reluctant subject as yourself.
While earnest biographers forge down your trail, you will
always elude them, smiling at their bungling efforts like a
hero outwitting the Keystone Cops.

I can't write a tribute. For one thing, a tribute to
L.T. is a contradiction in terms. You can't praise a humble
person; they don't like it. Besides, tributes are doomed to
failure since their goal is misguided: To idealize rather than
to tell the truth. I don't know the truth but I'll tell what I
do know and we'll see how it turns out. Some of the facts
are no doubt inaccurate. That's why this is a reminiscence
rather than a biography.

Louise Talma was born in France, the daughter of
a singer and her coach. Her father died when she was a
baby and at the age of eight, Louise took over his role of
accompanying her mother on the piano. We don't know
what effect such circumstances have on the Oedipal
complex.

From the start, music was central to L.T.'s life but
it was also a demanding companion. L.T.'s mother didn't
allow her child to ride a bike, for instance, for fear she
would injure her hands. In fact, for much of L.T.'s life, the
sacrifices demanded by music and those demanded by her
mother get fused. It seems almost obvious that a woman of

L.T.'s generation and single-mindedness would not marry. And in fact, L.T. lived with and supported her mother until she died when L.T. was thirty-five.

From the time she was about five, L.T. went with her mother to eight concerts a week. Her mother supported this habit by ghost-writing reviews, a practice which was common then and which gives a new twist to the phrase, "freedom of the press." L.T. kept up this pace of concert going until she was well into her eighties. I went with her to some of these concerts and became an expert L.T. spotter at others. With her braid pinned up on one side and her friend, Alice Hufstader, next to her in a hat with a pheasant feather rising from it, they were easy to spot. At intermission, Mrs. Hufstader would get up to scan the crowd and report on her findings or L.T. would go out and have a cigarette.

In her twenties, L.T. toyed with the idea of becoming a chemist. This was her "wild oats" period and that's about as wild as it got, so far as anyone knows. (There was a rumor when I was at Hunter, that she had dated Charles Ives. I'm more inclined to believe the rumor that she hated his music.) Perhaps she was intrigued by combining chemicals to make new concoctions as she had been intrigued by combining notes to make new harmonies. Anyway, this deviation from her straight and narrow musical path ended around the time she was hired, without a college degree, to teach music at Hunter College. She stayed there for over fifty years, recruiting Boulanger graduates for the faculty and turning the department into one of the best in the country. Somehow, she managed to get along with the musicologists as well, although she harbors a skepticism about their discipline for the same reason I distrust advice on childrearing from people who have never had children.

As a teacher, she was not for the faint of heart. She seemed to come as close as a human being could to God: Like Him, she had the air of knowing everything but she wasn't telling.

Having few foibles herself, she wasn't tolerant of them in others. It was almost eerie to see her read the future from a single act as though it was a molecule of DNA, bearing the secret of an entire personality. Once, when a student made a careless mistake, L.T. told him that if there was ever a group outing, she wouldn't go in a car he was driving.

Of course, both in her music and in her life, she herself is consistent as the Mass. (The only exception I know of is that although her manuscripts are impeccable, she claims her apartment would be a mess without the maid. I find that hard to believe.) She embodies integrity with emphasis on the "grit." When she gets an idea, she starts on it immediately and stays the course. Others may divorce, have crises and abandon careers to go fishing. L.T. has composed every summer of her life, either at Fontainebleau or at some artists' colony. Her goals are far-sighted: works of art that survive us.

Although she would never stoop to think in such terms, she is the paragon of the liberated woman. She has done what she wanted, according to what she believes in, regardless of what anyone else might say. And, several generations ahead of her time, she does it without fanfare.

About what she believes in: In music, it is those harmonies and forms that provided the basis and basses of all music from c. 1600-1914: the Trinity of tonic, dominant and subdominant. It is probably no coincidence that she also has three suits that she has rotated for about eight months of the year for twenty years.

Her ideals are the highest and her ideas, it seems at times, carved of granite. Such people make great artists and lousy jurors. I remember discussing with her an article in the New Yorker about a painter who was indicted for painting realistic $5 bills. He wasn't using them for money but he was violating a law which forbade copying money. L.T. said the case was ridiculous and he wasn't guilty. In fact the law, as it was written, may indeed have been ridiculous but he was also almost certainly violating it. L.T. said that was irrelevant and if she was on the jury, she would make up her own mind. Until then, I hadn't realized the unlikely faces vigilanteism can wear.

Then there was the question of spinach. One day, I picked L.T. up from St. Thomas More's and we went to lunch. Her dish came with a side order of spinach which she offered me because she didn't like it. We were discussing homosexuality, an idea which appalled L.T. I attempted to show it to her in another light.

"Could you make yourself want this spinach?" I asked.

"I don't see what that has to do with it," she answered. "I eat spinach when I have to." (Actually, it was cucumbers but that vegetable is too evocative, given the context.)

As resolutely as she dismissed some people, she championed others. While M.S. was studying with Nadia Boulanger in Paris, he received $100 from L.T. with a note explaining that the money came from a fund for students in his position. Since such a fund had never been heard of before but since, also, L.T. never lies, the only explanation for this manna of money is that she created the fund herself, contributed its only contents and disbursed them.

Despite her lofty ideals and impatience with imperfection, she has a keen interest in human frailty, at least, from a distance. For instance, she loves reading other people's mail. Usually only great people's, it's true, and then only when it's been published so that it's no longer mail but correspondence. Her own letters, at least the ones to me, are guarded, as though to thwart any readers with inclinations similar to her own.

There's a facial expression L.T. has and I would give a great deal to know where it comes from. It's an elusive smile which is basically kindly but is also capable of taking on a knowing gleam at the recognition of human weakness. I used to hear it when I would call her from Saudi Arabia and it sustained me during the year and a half my father was dying, reminding me that outside the hospital halls, life went on and was good.

Over the years I've written L.T. many letters from

different parts of the world. I told her of dark things and wonderful things and if these letters still existed, they would make great blackmail material. (Update following her death: Upon inquiry, Russell Oberlin, the counter-tenor who was in charge of her estate, assured me they did not.) When I heard from her after she'd received one, I'd hear the smile that said, "These things come and go. From where I sit, they're like the frantic running around of ants."

Whether we like it or not, all of us become known to some extent. We leave traces even by what we don't say or do. L.T., of course, is very wise. Her trail is her music and I don't dare speak of that since it speaks beautifully for itself. In fact, the tribute L.T. would most appreciate would be a concert of her work. Everything else will eventually be forgotten, but not so long as there are people around who know her.

Addendum: I'm happy to report that my observation that Louise Talma would elude biographers is proving all wet: The musicologist Kendra Preston Leonard's Louise Talma: A Life in Composition will be published by Ashgate Publishing in 2014.

Part Two:
Around Town

Rosamund Bernier

During my early twenties, I had a series of low-level jobs: Waitress, salesperson, you name it. They were all demeaning – people don't often bother to be civil to those they consider beneath them and any thought of sustained conversation or real friendliness with the clientele was naive.

But there was a hierarchy among these dead-end positions, in terms, say, of whether they were what my grandmother called "sit-down jobs" or whether they offered perks such as use of the phone. And one of them was fun: ushering lectures at the Metropolitan Museum. Staying behind after all the visitors had gone home, a lowly drone could psych herself into feeling a frisson of privilege: Once, I gate-crashed the opening of an Egyptian exhibit. In black and white usher's get-up, I fit right in.

The lecturers themselves ranged from unmemorable to boring except for one: Rosamund Bernier. She was reknowned in those rarefied circles that pay attention to art historians.

The first night of her series, there was a sense of emergency in the air. Princess Margaret was attending and security was tight. Doris, the head usher, usually a relaxed woman who hung out with us whenever we went for drinks after work, gave instructions with military authority. I was assigned the position of ticket collector at the bottom of the escalator.

At a quarter to eight, the audience arrived in Armani

suits or long dresses and furs, presented their tickets to be torn and glided up the escalator. The process was going smoothly until a woman wafted in wearing a sky-blue gown that made her look like someone's fairy godmother. She was escorted by a man in a tuxedo.

When I asked for her ticket, she gestured vaguely around her neck. I thought, "Poor thing; she's mute," and didn't press the matter. These were not people with whom you put up a fight.

Once everyone was in, we locked the entrance and proceeded upstairs. The lights went out. In the dark, diamonds glittered like the eyes of animals in the woods.

Bernier swept on.

She was, of course, wearing a sky-blue gown.

With lyrical eloquence, she rhapsodized about painters and kings in whose company she seemed to belong for in her dazzling dress, one could imagine her, say, serving as interior designer to the court of François I. The audience was enraptured.

After the lecture, I went up to her.

"When you gestured around your throat, I thought you were mute," I said. "I am very pleased to see that you're not."

She laughed with the charm of Glenda, the Good Witch of the North, as played by Billie Burke.

All of her lectures were transcendent but at least as mesmerizing was the pageant of her gowns. They all had the same cut as the first – the drama lay in the succession of colors: The second week, the gown was purple; the week after that, white; the fourth week, black.

I wondered what she could possibly do for the last lecture to top this escalation of colors.

It was gold.

The Don as Teacher: William Hickey's Other Role

For a couple of years after college, I chose music for soap operas. It was a dispiriting job. The music didn't come from the great works we'd studied as undergraduates but was bland, canned Muzak tailored to specific scene categories: "Tension," "romantic,""neutral." The scripts, too, churned out at the rate of an hour's worth a day, were destined for mediocrity.

I was frustrated with the job which could have been performed equally well by a musically literate sixteen-year-old. The star system at work didn't help matters either. Laying claim to neither the panache of the "talent" – directors, actors, production staff – nor the muscle of the unions, music supervisors fell between the cracks of the studio hierarchy to the lowest point on the totem pole.

But people find interest where they can and in the course of the job, I came to admire the actors who had to call on their deeper selves from six in the morning until six at night or later, depending on the complexity (i.e. number of cast members for the director to shuffle around) in a given day's show.

A couple of them, however, were downright bad. This didn't give me cause for contempt; I could relate. I, too, would not have been able to cry or get angry on cue. But more important than empathy, watching the bad actors gave me hope. Actors made real money and got respect too.

I decided to take acting lessons, enrolling in an

introductory class taught by William Hickey at Herbert Berghof Studios, no audition required.

I soon learned how out of place my motives for being there – greed and narcissism – were. The other students in the class, most of whom had studied acting before, went through profound soul searching before even reading the script aloud. This acting business wasn't as easy as it looked and I realized with cold dread that I was a fraud who didn't belong. Meanwhile, however, Hickey himself was so pithy that I also came to understand my true purpose in being in that class: to preserve his words.

I didn't know who would be interested in reading about him but when he died, I sent the resulting article to the woman who had been listed in his obituary as his survivor.

She sent back a kind letter along with Grace Glueck's book about Brooklyn (my return address) from Hickey's library. It's an engaging trove of anecdotes (writer Silvia Fine Kaye's dentist father waived payment when he treated members of the mob) that happens also to contain, whether coincidentally or not, a picture of a house on Monroe Place which had been used in Prizzi's Honor, the movie that had made Hickey's career.

"All right, what did you go for?"

It is two P.M. We are in the basement of Herbert Berghof studios where William Hickey is about to comment on the first performance of the afternoon's class.

On a stool across the stage from the two young actors

who have just performed a scene from Shakespeare's As You Like It, Hickey's leprechaun-like figure rocks and nods rhythmically as he listens to the answer. A match flares to ignite the first of the afternoon's many cigarettes.

"Well, in the beginning I was preoccupied, thinking about Rosalind."

The young actor's eyes cast about restlessly, unseeing, for an answer within himself.

"What I really had trouble with, though, was trying to justify standing there and asking her all those questions: 'Who does time gallop withal?' and all that. If I were in that situation, I would get very impatient with so much banter."

"Uh huh." Hickey continues to nod and chew his cigarette.

He is small as a chimney sweep and dressed like one, in black and various shades of dirt. He loathes washing and therefore, the rain. For years typecast as a derelict or drunk, he more recently played the upholder of family pride, the most princely of the Prizzi clan in Prizzi's Honor.

At the moment, hunched in simian attitude, he looks like a gargoyle surveying human folly on the stage below his perch. But his eyes pierce the Dickensian smoke of the room, as well as the psyches of his actors, with the intensity of a laser.

"She dazzles you. 'Who is this?'" he asks as Orlando. "'It's a boy, but what a boy!'

'You say you're preoccupied when you come on. But who are you?"

He pauses between observations to allow them to sink in while he lights another cigarette. "The Statue of Liberty may be preoccupied but she is still the Statue of Liberty.

'The actor's work is in the beginning – how to walk on. Everything else, the author wrote."

Nodding in recognition, the acolyte listens with the attention one might bestow on a gifted fortune teller.

"Art is the opposite of life. In life we never know the end. In art, we know the end but never the beginning.

'As for you!" Hickey fixes his gaze on Rosalind. "This is a disgrace. I've seen you improvise and I know you can do better than what you showed us here. If you took this to an audition they'd say, 'It's interesting,' and they'd see you had some sense of style but that isn't all I want – from *you*."

A girl who is to perform later in the class rummages through her backpack for a prop.

"Quiet!" Hickey shouts out of courtesy to his two performers as much as in delight at startling the audience of students.

Rosalind is not among those affected by his outburst.

"I want more than that too," she pleads with tearful conviction.

"Do it again and this time think about what you're saying. Don't prance around the stage so much. I'll probably miss what you're doing now but then you can put it back in later. Is that enough to go on?"

The actress nods and gathers up her sword and

costume-bag with the efficient gestures of one who is determined to exit with her dignity intact.

The studio is long and divided into ad hoc performance and audience sections. Deep in the dark expanse of backstage, behind a curtain, are kept props and a few pieces of furniture that turn up in nearly every scene: a door in a frame; a chest of drawers supporting a mirror; flea market china.

For the present scene, the actor performing a monologue from Richard III has put out several grey papier maché boulders to indicate a bleak terrain. Leaping among them, he grinds his teeth between the immortal words as though hungry with vicious visions. When his speech is finished, he looks over at Hickey, eyes still flashing like a clash of daggers. Hickey gestures him towards the customary chair.

"Why did you choose to do it that way?" he asks.

"I didn't choose to – It just happened," the actor explains in triumph.

"Well, who do you think did it to you?" Hickey retorts rhetorically. "The great ventriloquist in the sky?

'All I want is for you to be you. I don't want how you think the character should be feeling at any particular time. The way you're feeling is the way the character feels and I don't give a fuck about interpretation or anything else. Excuse me. I mean that in the spiritual sense of the word." He bows in exaggerated apology.

"I don't care if you do this again or do something else but take it slowly. Quiet!" he barks at the girl in high-heeled boots carrying her props up for the next scene.

"Sorry," she mutters.

"I doubt it," Hickey snaps.

The actress casts back a look of hurt annoyance and disappears behind the curtain.

Hickey turns to the audience and whispers conspiratorially, "I'm trying to get her mad at me before she does this scene." He returns to the villainous king who is following him with the enthusiasm of a game-show M.C.

"It doesn't matter if we're here all day waiting for something to happen. If nothing happens, fine. 'Nothing' is fascinating."

Prepared for any challenge the actor leaves, unfazed even by the prospect of coming face to face with Nothing.

"The quality of mercy" follows, delivered by Virginia, the girl whom Hickey has been trying to annoy.

She is tall and disheveled, with the air of someone who hasn't fully woken up. The previous week, Hickey assigned her the role of Portia as a contrast to those she has always chosen herself: depressed cocktail waitresses and waifs.

She conveys the monologue simply, with sincerity and even, to everyone's surprise, clarity. When it is over, Hickey speaks quietly.

"First of all I want to say, that's the best acting I've ever seen you do. Did you have someone in mind for Shylock?"

"Yes."

"May I ask who?" Hickey does not shy away from

questions that might shed light on how his students work. On the contrary, his curiosity is the sort most often found among great people and boors.

"My ex-husband. He was a very hard, unforgiving man."

"Can't you think of Shylock as someone to be won over? After all, he hasn't had an easy life. He's been discriminated against.

'If we try to show what's wrong with something, we have no show." He nods as though to encourage a nod in response, to goad his listener into understanding. "Lillian Hellman once said she didn't like writing about the theatre because theatrical anecdotes were always about disasters: 'The time I pulled the door-knob and the door came with me and I had to spend the whole scene holding it up.' Actually, these are achievements; you did it!

'Now get her the hook." He waves at no one in particular. "I want to see Abbie and Ron."

The pair summoned have chosen a scene from what appears as frequently in acting classes as potatoes at English school lunches: A Streetcar Named Desire.

The scene opens innocently with Stella arranging a birthday party for her sister Blanche. The actress playing Stella is a lovely, dark girl with large eyes and round limbs. She is wearing a pillow under her dress to show Stella is pregnant and as she fusses around the kitchen, humming, she creates a cozy scene.

Her husband Stanley enters, mumbling with a listlessness that is unusual for this actor. Ordinarily, he has a robust stage presence which he is not ashamed to throw into his roles. I wonder if he's emulating the understated approach of Brando, who first played the role, but is exaggerating it as he tends to exaggerate everything.

When the scene is over, Hickey addresses Stella first.

"Do you think that thing makes you pregnant?"

"Stella" laughs. "I thought this might help me feel what it's like carrying a baby around. I–"

"Don't give me that," Hickey interrupts. "That's just actor stuff.

'There's a scene in St. Joan where the archbishop says to her, 'My child, you are falling in love with religion.' And now I say to you, 'My child, you are falling in love with acting.'

'What are you trying to do in this scene? If you want to be Stella, don't stuff yourself with a pillow. Do what she's doing. If you want to play my life, don't act like me. Try to do what I'm trying to do. Anything else is imitation which is jerking off. And I mean that in the *dirty* sense of the word." He savors the word "dirty" with the delight of a preacher describing the details of Hell.

"And you!" he shouts to Ron. "What do you think you're doing up there?"

"You told me last time to stop walking around so much. So I tried to tone the whole thing down, I guess."

"Whatever I told you, it doesn't work. Any suggestion I make is intended to help you. If instead it kills what you had before, then don't take it. Acting should never make us less than we are. It should make us more.

You can gamble, throw Stella around, celebrate the world...
The only thing the actor has to be afraid of is the feeling
of, 'Oh my God, I'm going on and I don't give a shit.'
Capisc?"

The actors nod with restrained enthusiasm. Hickey
has given them something more useful than praise.

The final scene of the afternoon is from Birdbath,
a play about a young writer who becomes intrigued by a
misfit girl. In his apartment, she refuses his offer of a drink
and avoids his questions, talking instead about her mother
whom, we later learn, she has just killed.

The girl's part should be a good shelter for this
novice actress whose nerves and inhibitions can be used
to her advantage. However, they're not. As the scene
is drawn out to a pace that would try the patience of a
monument, we feel the actress' agony a little too keenly.

"All right, what did you go for?" Hickey addresses
the actor who is playing the writer.

"Well, I thought she was really different, but I started
to get exasperated when she didn't understand my desire to
write. I mean, it's my life..."

"But why can't that in itself be fascinating to you?
After all, how many times do you meet someone as naive
as she is? How refreshing it would be to find someone who
knew absolutely nothing as opposed to the rest of us who
all know the same goddamn stuff. You could think, '*Here's*
something to write about.' You could be nuttier than she
is."

The actor smiles slightly at the array of possibilities

the suggestion presents.

"How about you?" Hickey asks the ignorant matricide. "What problems did you have, if any?"

"I felt really uncomfortable; I couldn't get all the nuances we had in rehearsal. I was just waiting for it all to be over."

"I got a great compliment once, from a friend of mine who sat in on one of my classes. She said, 'I've been to other acting classes. They were like productions. Yours was a mess.'

'I don't want you to be comfortable. I'll get you a nice, comfortable coffin.

'We are living in an era when people discuss their libidos with a bus driver. If you're uncomfortable, you should be proud of it."

"It was worst in the middle," the girl goes on, not convinced. "I didn't know if I should be as shy as in the beginning or if I should begin to like him or if I was supposed to think about what I'd done to my mother."

"Never mind what you're feeling. What are you trying to do? To *him*? 'Drama' in Greek means 'action.' When we divide a scene into beats, it's not according to what we feel, it's according to the events that take place.

'Did you ever hear the story of Solomon Grundy?" Hickey recites: "Born on Monday, christened on Tuesday, married on Wednesday, sick on Thursday, worse on Friday, died on Saturday, buried on Sunday and that's the story of Solomon Grundy.' Never felt a thing."

The caretaker of the school has appeared at the door

to notify us that the building is closing. The class, listed on the schedule as two hours, is finally over after four, at least, officially. Hickey leaves with his last two performers in tow, talking on the stairs as they head out. In the street, darkness and a cold rain are descending but the trio and much of the rest of the class huddle around as Hickey continues to teach.

Marilyn Langner

1975

Marilyn Clark Langner is an actress, producer and, though much against her will, a writer. She is married to Philip Langner with whom she runs the Theatre Guild, a company founded by Philip's father, Lawrence, which first introduced O'Neill, Williams and other American greats to the stage. More recently the Guild has produced Golda, American Jubilee and Alan Ayckbourne's Absurd Person Singular. It also organizes cruises with a theatrical as well as a maritime crew aboard.

Langner has been in the theatre all her life:

"I first decided to be an actress when my older cousin said that's what she was going to do.

'I grew up in Long Beach, California, which wasn't the most stimulating community as far as theatre goes. It wasn't poverty-stricken; it was just Dullsville. Nixon country starts a little further up, just over the county line.

'My mother was a buyer for a large store and she used to go to New York quite frequently on business. She would always see as many plays as she could on these trips and used to bring home the playbills. She saw You Can't Take it With You, Life With Father... I remember all the titles very well; you'll see why in a moment. She used to describe the plays to me, using the cast of characters to help her remember but she never bothered too much with details. She would just say, 'That one was a professor. She was the landlady and I think he was just a plumber.'

I guess that was enough to get me started. I saw no reason why the plays wouldn't work just as well in Long Beach so I talked some of my friends into putting them on and I wrote them. If I found at the end of the script that I had left out three characters from the cast list, I would simply have them all come in at the same time as a trio.

'Everyone had heard of the Broadway hit of whatever we were doing at the moment and they came to our show expecting more or less the same play even though the actors would be about ten years old on average. We were very successful. We passed the hat at the end.

'It was all highly illegal and unethical. Now that I think about it, I don't know how my mother could have let me get away with it except that both she and my father were salespeople – my father was a Willy Loman type with all the problems, the sadness, that go along with it – so a good hustle was always appreciated in the house. Still, my mother must have cringed when she heard me talking to someone who had just come back from New York where they'd seen I Remember Mamma and I would say, 'Oh yes, I'm working on a script for that right now.'"

"Where did the money go?" I asked.

"I kept it. I suppose we had some staging expenses but we saved on publicity. Whatever was left over went to the cast and myself.

'Our biggest hit was probably You Can't Take it With You. That ran for about three weeks. Our audience came mostly from a nearby nursing home and they would all come every night. Probably they didn't hear well so it didn't get too boring. We got bored, though. About two weeks into the run, we started rehearsals for the next show.

'One of our less successful productions was about a black woman who had to overcome a mountain of problems that arose from being black. Blackness was unmentionable in Long Beach then so we made her white. Apart from that, the play was basically the same except that it was never too clear what her problem was.

'I also staged and wrote Aida. I don't recall being aware at the time that it was an opera. It came as a great shock when I finally saw the original several years later.

'I still find it disconcerting when agents come to Philip with some actress they want him to cast and say things like, 'She's marvelous; she just played Long Beach.'"

"How long did it take you to write the plays?"

"A night, maybe two. I hadn't yet taken any typing courses.

'By the time I reached junior high school, my parents were worried that I was a little too serious about the theatre so I had to go into something respectable. Since the only thing my family had ever done was sell, I started selling things too. I sold date-palms because I could get them for free. I'd climb up onto the wall of somebody's vine and cut off the date-palms and sell them. I never thought of it as stealing; I always sold them to the person whose vine I had taken them from. I thought it was immoral to sell them to somebody else. I did this until the customers found out where I'd acquired the palms.

'The other thing I did around that time was lend money. At very high interest rates. That's illegal too, isn't it? There was an ice-cream vendor who used to come around the school at lunch-time and I would set up my booth near him to lend dimes to anybody who needed them. The interest rate was ten percent. That's a penny. Per day. It was also a very good way to meet men. Girls, for some reason, were never so interested in any of this as boys. They were too well organized. Boys liked the business aspect of it and they wanted the ice-cream, too.

'It looked very impressive, me surrounded by twenty boys – especially if you weren't aware of the usury going on. I made about ten dollars on that operation. For the whole thing, that is.

'I've also invented a number of potentially useful items. A long time ago, I invented a toothbrush with dental floss coming out of the end. I took the bobbin of a sewing machine, wound the dental floss around it and attached it to the other end. It worked very well but the toothbrush would have to be longer than average. Johnson and Johnson were interested in it."

"Have you ever thought about writing a book?"

"Never. The experience of writing American Jubilee was so shattering, I'd never want to go through anything like it again.

'It really came out of the Rotterdam. There are usually about thiry-five performers on board and we all get very close – except for people like D. F. who shall remain nameless, who are impossible to work with. We always write something just for the cruise and this time, we decided to do songs with Viennese harmonies and jazz rhythms.

'I never intended to write it but I ended up having to do some of the lyrics.

'I hated the pressure, the self-judgment and the nasty money business that were all part of the professional theatre. You forget your priorities. We weren't in it anymore for that sense of, 'What if...?' or 'Let's play like...' that we used to have in Long Beach. I couldn't write in that deadly serious situation and anything that came out at all was forced and sounded it.

'At the same time, I was in Absurd. I lived in constant fear that when I went on stage, someone would notice that my eyes were red from crying. When I got home at night, I would feel my breasts for lumps. I usually managed to find something. Then I would say," – she acted out the scene with the excitement of a scientist who's discovered a new element – "I've found a lump! I think it's cancer!

'I started seeing a psychiatrist but I wasn't too good at that, either. I could never get the hang of stream of consciousness. The psychiatrist kept insisting anyone could do it and I kept not being able to. Finally, I got him to demonstrate. He said, 'You see that lamp beside you? When I look at that lamp, I think of the day my wife and I bought it. It was raining and that reminds me of a day when I was little and it was raining. I fell and got my pants wet.'

'So I agreed to try. I looked at the lamp and said, 'When I look at that lamp, I think of the day you and your wife bought it and it was raining...'"

"But in spite of all that, American Jubilee was a hit," I reminded her.

"I suppose so. We were stunned when Clive Barnes wrote that we had a lovely show. A lot of people called it an 'attractive production.' That was about the strongest adjective we got."

"Does the Theatre Guild do any standard repertory on the ship?"

"Oh yes. A few years ago, we did Slaves. One of the crew, – the *real* crew – was Turkish. As he was helping us load the equipment on board, he asked us what it was for and we told him it was for Slaves. His eyes lit up. He thought we were going to trade them."

"Do you plan to act again?"

"I just finished a movie in Missouri. It's going to be shown at the Cannes Film Festival. But I don't go to those Equity things anymore that are so democratic and embarrassing. Life gets easier as you get older. I'm much closer now than I was twenty years ago to that spirit of freedom we had in Long Beach."

Quentin Crisp

I first met Quentin Crisp when I wrote him a
fan letter saying he should get the Nobel Prize but the
Committee would probably not go for the idea. His
response included his home phone number. Delighted
to take the hint, I invited him to dinner (at my mother's
apartment) and, ever willing to tuck into a free meal, he
came for the first of what were to be many memorable
evenings.

My mother and I planned the guest lists for these
events with care to include people who would not drown
out the incomparable conversationalist. (He once described
a Mafioso acquaintance as "big as a tree and twice as
shady.") It always provided a frisson of excitement to see
his cape flung across the bed beneath his signature fedora
and cane, as though Oscar Wilde was in the next room (a
comparison which would have induced from Quentin a
polite groan.)

That first dinner took place in the middle of January
so, fearful he would chicken out because of the snow,
I picked him up in a cab. There was no doorbell to the
rooming house which that master of style holed up in; you
had to call from the phone booth across the street, next to
Hell's Angels headquarters.

His digs were barely a cut above homelessness: the
kitchen, a hot plate; the bathroom, down the hall. The brief
passage into the room was so narrow as to require entering
sideways, as though one were being born. The furniture

consisted of a bed and The Chair, a lopsided thing which was probably missing a leg.

Perhaps he was taken aback to be escorted by a young woman to an unknown apartment because during the whole cab ride uptown, he never once looked at me. (I believe in his long, colorful history were a few women who had thrown themselves at him.) This didn't stop me from looking at him, however. The surprising impression was that his make-up was not more glamorous. It was as if, in aspiring to a woman's look, he aimed not for Marlene Dietrich but for suburban ladies' luncheon.

Once we arrived, he did warm to my brother but apart from that, he didn't seem to take people in. He was a performer at the deepest level and if one didn't accept that, one missed the point of the experience.

A few years later, I had a talk show on Cable TV and he was my first guest. He loved being on television – it's how he regained his "virginity" as per his book, How to Become a Virgin – and was an interviewer's dream. (Naively, I thought I now understood the process and prepared the same number of questions for the following week's guest, Fran Lebowitz. But her style of humor is the opposite of his, laconic enough so that the novice host shook as she riffled her notes off camera to come up with her next question.)

He was so profoundly impersonal that one can't help wondering: Did anyone ever see beneath the mask? Did he?

Have You Got What It Takes To Be Hip?

Boom chicka boom chicka... Welcome to Sensation. No, it's not a new fragrance. Sensation is the new exhibit at the Brooklyn Museum that's been causing all this, well, sensation around town. The exhibit that asks questions – questions like, "They call this art?" "Can that metal detector detect plastique?" "How can I use my transfer to get home?" With something to offend prudes and animal rights activists alike.

Here is a shark suspended in 5% formaldehyde, prophetic of the dead animals that lie waiting for us in the rooms ahead. How scary he would be if he were alive! But he isn't so... What are we supposed to think? Is what we think the art? Mmm... Looks like maybe it is. Is that a cop out? You bet!

Boom tacka boom boom. Here is a picture consisting, (in lovely colors,) of the artist's written comments on contemporary life: Comedians, pop music, da dah, da dah. They're not interesting or original but this is art not literature so that's not the point, Genius.

Tikki tikki bing bong. Here is an empty room. But no, look! There's an arrangement sort of like a mini-Stonehenge on the floor. Maybe that's to remind us the exhibit is from England. But it's too neat and boring. Maybe it's Stonehenge if a modern artist were to redo it. And those aren't stones; they're a hundred little lavender cubic thingies. Please walk around the art work rather than through it so you don't trip on it. But wait, they're not exactly cubic. Let's check the title; in this exhibit, half the art is in the explanation... They're models of the spaces beneath chairs! A must for the art collector with a big empty room or a hundred chairs arranged in rows of ten with the right sized spaces under them.

La la shooo... Now the prize piece of the collection, behind plexiglass which stands several feet in front of the picture so if you want to throw a rotten egg at it, just step a little to the left: Chris Ofili's controversial rendition of the Holy Virgin with a breast of elephant dung. Well, I'm sorry to disappoint you but whatever else this exhibit is, it's not sacreligious. The way you can know is: In another picture, Mr. Ofili lovingly inscribes into a similar mound of elephant dung the names of Miles Davis and other jazz greats. Nobody has suggested he's defiling *them*. Try to get this through your head: Mr. Ofili is, if you'll pardon the expression, into elephant dung. He gets it from the London zoo and puts it everywhere. And in case anybody's told you that you can't tell it's elephant dung, they're wrong. You can. At least, you can tell it's some kind of dung. I'm not up on the varieties so I don't know if Mr. Ofili shaped these baseball-sized piles or if they came this way. But if you didn't know what they were you'd say, "Is that horse shit or something?" This in turn leads to other provocative questions: How much modern art is horse shit? What about the pieces in this exhibit?

But if you have any doubts about what this exhibit means, just listen to the sound track narrated by David Bowie that introduces each of these commentaries. It'll convince you: It may not be art but boy, is it contemporary.

Um, Parlez-Vous Engelska?

Sometimes Americans travelling abroad get a nasty surprise: Not everyone they meet speaks English. Often, of course, the natives we run into speak English better than we do. In Amsterdam, for instance, an old lady feeding the pigeons gave me such articulate directions, I immediately pegged her as a CIA operative. And a wandering eccentric muttering to himself proved on closer inspection to be reciting Chaucer. This cosmopolitanism can be intimidating to one who secretly wishes there was a need to whip out the phrase book and order Dutch Split Pea Soup in Dutch.

But off the tourist-beaten track, this can, in fact, occasionally be necessary. There still are places where one needs not only to do as the Romans do but also speak as the Romans speak, though most of them are well outside of Rome. With these places in mind, I feel justified in packing a small phrase book to study on the train.

I harbor another kind of fantasy as well, when travelling. I imagine wandering, as happened to a friend of mine in North Africa, onto, say, a military base and landing in a situation fraught with misunderstanding and danger. And so, while the effort usually ends up as so much excess baggage, still I study my phrase book with the intensity of someone learning CPR.

My anxiety is soon rewarded. In fact, reading phrase books can quickly become a hypnotic activity for one in a frame of mind as susceptible as mine to dire suggestion.

For the authors have a bent for the disastrous that hovers gratifyingly on the edge of paranoia: These compact bibles contain every mishap likely to befall the most ill-fated visitor.

Often, as in the Italian text before me now, the opening sentence reads, "Is there anyone here who speaks English?"

With a bit of luck, the answer to that will obviate the need for the rest of the chapter. But if it's No, the hapless tourist will have to read on:

I do not speak Italian.
I've lost my way.
What are you saying?
I can't find my wallet.
I've been robbed.
Call the police.

The gamut of human drama rests within these slim volumes. Thus by page two of the same Italian text, we have reached a degree of emergency rivaled only by soap opera synopses:

Help!
Fire!
I am an American.
Take me to the American Consulate.
I've left my overcoat on the train.
I cannot find my hotel.

I've lost my passport.
I cannot find my husband/wife/son/daughter.

Wiped out by these events, I am relieved by the title of the next chapter, "Miscellaneous Encounters," until I spot the subheading: *At the Police Station.* The ensuing dialogue is, as ever, in the bare-bones style of life's less charming moments:

You are under arrest.
I want a lawyer.
This is your last warning. Etc.

Of course, the texts also deal with the banal necessities of travel. But even these passages are written with the authors' ever world-weary eye and have a sinister subcurrent:

Customer: This room is too small. How much is the larger one?
Manager: The weekly rate is 10,000,000 lire.
Customer: Do you have something cheaper?
Manager: No, and I must inform you that you pay in advance.
Customer: I will pay for two nights and that is all.

But of course, it is not only the action-packed scenes that may cause a reader to lose herself in a language text; it is also the aesthetic pleasure of finding order in what previously seemed like chaos, i.e., the joy of learning a few phrases of a foreign language. This delight is heightened by hope. For linguists assure us that the more languages one studies, the easier the study of languages gets. Once one masters one foreign language, they imply, its friends and relations follow soon behind.

Take, for instance, the passive voice. Anyone who has studied a Romance language knows that the passive (as in, "My car was stolen, my wallet snatched and my house, set on fire,") may be expressed by the reflexive, ("I pour myself a drink.") Thus we can translate a sign in a shop window that proclaims, "Se Habla Espanol," whether or not we have ever studied Spanish. *"Spanish is spoken!"* it cries and not, *"Spanish speaks itself,"* or, *"He speaks Spanish to himself."* And this can be surprisingly reassuring – like the appearance of an acquaintance at a party of strangers – if the shop in question is in Central Uzbekistan.

Ode Upon Getting to the Bus-Stop in Time to Watch Two Busses Go Lumbering Off Together into the Sunset

Is it so that we may choose?
Is that why busses come in twos?
Whatever bus you see at random
Always seems to be in tandem.
With this one would find nothing wrong
Were it not for the waiting periods between busses
Which are twice as long.

Neither snow nor hail nor sleet nor rain
Can part the faithful constant twain.
Let anxious commuters get colder and colder,
When the busses finally arrive, they are shoulder to
shoulder
As though each were a Siamese brother.
You can't have one without the other.

This close rapport 'twixt bus and bus
Might begin to bore the rest of us
Save when, to liven up our lives
They come in threes or fours or fives.

The Princess of the Jury

There's a sort of anonymous intimacy on jury duty —
like that of passengers in a railway carriage who, during the
night, find themselves asking, "Sorry, did I kick your ear?"
On jury duty, people think they'll never see you again so
they don't put on airs.

When I was on jury duty, I met an older woman
whom I shall call Mrs. K. Over lunch the first day, Mrs.
K. told me she ran a non-profit cultural organization. The
second day, she revealed its purpose: To promote Russian
artists in the US and help people of Russian descent here
learn about their heritage. She was also involved in a
project that had something to do with Italy.

As the week wore on, details emerged about her past,
including the fact that she was an Italian princess. Her
husband had been an impoverished Russian aristocrat. He
had also been a difficult man. To escape her difficulties,
Mrs. K. had become a Theosophist which, if Wikipedia is
to be trusted, involves believing in air battles as well as
animal-human chimaeras between 200,000 and a million
years ago.[4] Perhaps it was a Theosophist whom I once
overheard in the Egyptian section of the Metropolitan
Museum say, "You know, the Egyptians were very
advanced. I understand they even had color television."

But even dearer to Mrs. K.'s heart than Theosophy
was Italy. When jury duty was over, she invited me to her
apartment to look at pictures of her castle in Tuscany.

She lived on Fifth Avenue at the same address,

she maintained, as Jackie O. The buildings in this neighborhood are discreet like men in suits whose appearance does not betray their billions. Inside, however, the apartments approach the dimensions and baroque craftsmanship of Versailles.

Mrs. K. led me into the library, a room with ornate molding around its 20-foot ceiling, sat down and crossed her legs. In her heavy black silk skirt and light blue silk blouse, she looked as though she was sitting for a portrait. The house-painter had been by that morning to give an estimate for the one room: $11,000. I imagined him taking one look around and blurting out the biggest number that popped into his mind.

I had given Mrs. K. a story I had written. She said I was a good writer because I had a large vocabulary. Inwardly cringeing, I made a mental note to use simpler words. Then she opened the family photograph album and started turning pages as I murmured polite comments. Eventually she reached a photograph of a large Hearstian castle.

"It's beautiful!" I exclaimed.

"That? That's our house in Newport. *This* is the castle." And she turned another page.

There it was, or at least, some of its three hundred rooms. It did indeed make the first house look like a grownup's mud pie.

"I used to think I was a poor child," Mrs. K. sighed. "All the other children at school had six hundred rooms in their castles."

She explained that the castle had hit hard times. These days, during the winter, it was overrun by peasants seeking shelter. But no one could take advantage of her – she had had them removed.

"Where did they go?" I asked.

"All over," she replied indignantly. "The halls, the bedrooms..."

"I mean, after you evicted them."

"Oh, I don't know," she shrugged. "Anyway, they're all descended from criminals."

But, she continued, she had managed to hang onto the castle's art treasures. Her favorite was a sculpture in the garden of the goddess Diana. A neighbor who had a statue of Venus had said that Venus reigned supreme among goddesses.

"Nonsense," Mrs. K. sniffed now. "Diana was a much more important goddess than Venus."

She ended the afternoon with a history lesson: It was tragic, she said, that history did not pay adequate homage to Marie Antoinette. She was a substantial intellect, not some flibbertygibbet as historians insisted – a feminist theory I'd have found more plausible coming from anyone else's mouth.

Update 2012: I don't know about Marie Antoinette's intellect but she certainly takes the rap for a situation over which she, being neither executive nor legislator, had no control. Mention the French Revolution, and if they know anything at all about it, students will cite the Queen rather than her husband who was the monarch with actual power at the time.

Nor, as it turns out, was she necessarily the author of the infamous line, "Let them eat cake." What's more:

"'Let them eat brioche' isn't quite as cold a sentiment as one might imagine. At the time, French law required bakers to sell fancy breads at the same low price as the plain breads if they ran out of the latter. The goal was to prevent bakers from making very little cheap bread and then profiting off the fancy, expensive bread. Whoever really said "'Let them eat brioche' may have meant that the bakery laws should be enforced so the poor could eat the fancy bread if there wasn't enough plain bread to go around."[5]

Sylvia

Sylvia's mother is manic-depressive; her father, a psychiatrist. When Sylvia was a child, her mother abused her while her father stood by passively and watched. When Sylvia was twelve, her mother broke a bottle of wine over her head. It was a christening of sorts. Sylvia ran away from home, to an aunt's house on her father's side. No one bothered to try to get her back.

Her father's side of the family had been missionaries and the uncle with whom she was now living was a minister. It makes sense, then, that Sylvia became religious. When I knew her, for about ten years starting when we were in our mid-twenties, she had the pensive air of a woman out of a painting by Vermeer. She also still looked like a teenager – the kind you would want to have babysit for your children – perhaps because she was determined to cling to her innocence.

She spoke of her adopted family, especially of a favorite aunt who made plum pancakes and had a Persian cat. In all her descriptions, however, she never mentioned that this aunt was a midget. (When I finally met the aunt, Sylvia explained that she had no ovaries.) The aunt liked children's books and I thought that she might be retarded but no; she was unusually intelligent. Sylvia herself worked with retarded people and for a brief time, unconsciously mirrored their mannerisms.

In an earlier age, Sylvia might have become a nun but six years ago she married a minister twenty years older than she and she now has three children.

George

My mother's brother was a fireman, fifteen years older than my mother. As a young man, he had educated himself but when he joined the fire department the other men made fun of his speech and he adopted theirs. He lived in the Bronx, took subways everywhere and, to my mother's frustration, kept all his savings in the bank. My mother's attitude to her brother was one of irritation at his lack of humor, lack of taste, lackadaisical manner and lack of mobility from the depressed condition of their youth.

When in his seventies he became ill, my mother gave him a subscription to the New York Times. He was moved by the thoughtfulness and, by his standards, the extravagance of the gift.

When he died, he left half a million dollars to his wife and daughter and several thousand to my mother. My mother missed him, among other things, for all the financial advice she had never obtained and which he could now never give. She looked for clues in his past as to how he had amassed this fortune – never mind why – but didn't find any. She did, however, revise her opinion of his lacks, particularly of humor.

Writer Wannabe Seeks Brush with Death

When I was five, I folded over a piece of paper, got an eyebrow pencil from my mother's make-up table and wrote a children's book. It began (and ended:) "Once upon a time, there was a long, long Queen." Soon after, school started and with it, the drama of friendship. Writing went into hibernation.

The summer before I turned ten, we moved to England. Looking back, homesick, I wrote a movie based on a book called The Bells of Bleecker Street about a gang of children in the Village. I'd only been to the Village once, for an avant-garde production of Rumpelstiltskin but I missed my gang of friends.

Writing a script was satisfying because it didn't take long to finish a page. I'd covered eleven pages when once more, school took over; writing dove underground.

We moved back to New York four years later. For the first time, I went to a private school. This school meant business. And its business, as far as I could see, was writing. Math was hard, but required only mathematical understanding. French and Latin were hard but required only memory. English was where we would prove the mettle of our soul.

The English teacher who was the artistic mastermind of the school cultivated lonely, poetic types. Consciously or not, she instilled in us these commandments: *Good work is dark, heavy, dredged up from the soggy depths of suffering. The artist offers her happiness as a sacrifice to the gods of Art. Go, thou and do likewise. Suffer and it'll all come out in the work.*

I set out to suffer. This wasn't hard at a school where friendship was seen as an obstacle to academic success. But writers were supposed to be unhappy. Surely I was on the right track for writing heavy, poetic stories, just what the English teacher ordered.

It didn't work out that way. For while she admired suffering as a source of inspiration, the English teacher recoiled if it bared itself too brazenly.

"Sometimes we have to rise above our own mundane lives," she told a girl who'd written about a love-hate relationship with food.

It seemed there were other commandments: *Draw not on thy own experience: too easy, self-absorbed. No one else will be interested. Thou shalt disguise thy loneliness as something else. Let us see only its shy form in the distance. Do not show it to us close up with its folds of flesh, its crying, craving craw.*

I froze over, numbed. *Draw not on thy own experience; it's too lowly to be of interest to anyone else...* What could I write that was high-falutin'?

We'd been reading Paradise Lost. In homage to Milton and the English teacher who revered him, I wrote a monologue by God. In it, God was angry at the state of the world. I wasn't angry at the state of the world but I knew there were things I should be angry about so I wrote about them. The assignment got a B. I wasn't angry enough.

Later, we were assigned to write a satire. (We'd

been reading Swift). I decided to satirize religion. Real writers were always satirizing it: Didn't Swift or Pope or somebody satirize the holiness professed by some congregants who wore lace and finery? Religion was a juicy yet lofty subject. I would get points just for thinking of it.

My family had never been to a religious service within my lifetime although my mother had a Catholic girlhood and my father probably had a bar mitzvah. To research the satire, I went to St. Thomas' on 53rd and 5th one Sunday morning and observed the congregation.

They didn't do anything offensive. They didn't come out of church and insult the homeless man leaning against the wall. Their clothes were probably fine but I'm not one of those people who can size up clothes, telling at a glance whether the seams will hold or the wool refrain from balling up or whatever it is that makes clothes "good." But if their clothes were fine, they weren't outrageously fine. I didn't see expensive jewelry flash but then, I'm no good at sizing up jewelry either. And I had the feeling expensive jewelry didn't flash.

This project was also doomed to mediocrity, of course. With a sigh for lack of a better idea, I invented finery for the congregation and haughty remarks for them to make to the homeless man. What else was there to do – satirize the English teacher? The school? I took both seriously.

I read widely, reading being an honorable way to avoid homework and essential to my writer's apprenticeship. One evening as I emerged, groggy, from a weekend with Hemingway, I decided that in order to have something to write about, a writer had to live dangerously. What I needed was an encounter with death. I was too cowardly to do anything about this realization but a few years later, life came through on its own.

I'd been out of college two years waiting tables by day, writing by night. I'd majored in Music and wanted my day job to be teaching Music Theory but that had turned out to be as quixotic a notion as writing. You needed a Ph. D. and I'd had it with school.

One empty day in August, Tanya called. Tanya was a family friend who'd woven in an out of our lives for the last twenty years; maybe more, I couldn't remember her that far back. She saw her role towards me as that of surrogate aunt. At my age, she'd been a struggling actress and she knew I was a struggling music teacher and writer. She wanted to help and an opportunity had come up.

An actor friend of hers, Robert C., needed someone to clean his house for the next three weekends. His regular housekeeper ("A bit of a dictator," Tanya said, "but tip-top at cleaning,") had gone home to Germany for the month. Robert was eccentric – Tanya described a few of the ways but they didn't sound alarming and the pay was eight dollars an hour, three dollars above the going rate as befitted a tip-top housekeeper.

Saturday morning at ten I rang the bell. No one answered. I tried again and waited. Then I knocked. As in a fairy-tale, the door to the apartment opened by itself at the touch. Cautiously, I went in. Propped against the hall mirror was a note: *Genevieve: Start in living-room. 2)Kitchen. 3)Vacuum cleaner in hall closet.*

I had my work cut out for me. As Tanya had described, the housekeeper hadn't been there in a week and the dog, Celine, hadn't been walked in four years. No one knew why. But Celine's shaky command of paper-training ensured that my salary, which had seemed a windfall on the phone, would be well-earned.

After picking up Celine's messes, I parted the shoes in the closet and pulled the vacuum cleaner from behind an overgrowth of coats. As it bumped over a sneaker, the bag fell out, spilling its most recent contents: a mass of dust packed into a cylinder, one dark blue sock, a nickel, two amyl nitrate wrappers.

Vacuuming the living-room, I lifted the skirt of the couch: Three more wrappers lay as though left by the tide. The vacuuming done, I fluffed the cushions; amyl nitrate capsules lay wedged between them.

Amyl nitrates appeared everywhere, like locusts: Rolling in the drawers or falling out of scripts, a volume of Auden and Robert's Rolodex. They were in the cupboards, among the teabags and under the kitchen sink next to the Brillo. In a set of china containers labeled Coffee, Sugar, Spices, they were Sugar.

At eleven, Robert shuffled into the living-room.

"Morning," he mumbled. It might have been a greeting or a curse.

Meeting Robert taught me that acting is like the lottery. The actors I knew back then went to class, worked out, hoped for a break and got nothing. Robert did as little as possible and got everything.

Not given to working out, he was bloated as Humpty Dumpty with wet lips that hung open, quivering, and sparse hair that sprouted like a pineapple's tuft. This didn't matter, however, because Robert did voice-overs. Even if Tanya hadn't told me, I would have instantly identified his voice as that of the T. cat food commercials.

He stumbled to the bar and poured himself a shot. I remembered that Tanya had also said he was an alcoholic. This, apparently, didn't matter either. For although he didn't show up at the studio until noon, he had what amounted to tenure: His voice, which could purr silkily, was unmistakably identified with T. So each year he made two hundred thousand dollars for a few days' work.

The kitchen sink was filled with dishes placed at perilous angles in what looked like a considered effort at randomness. The surplus lay on the counter and the drying rack. I couldn't figure out where the food had come from because the fridge was empty. Or rather, it had the trademark contents of the bachelor – a jar of olives, half a jar of mustard crusting at the rim, an opened bottle of wine.

I got to work on the dishes, a chore I avoided at home. But at Robert's, I scrubbed industriously. Not only was there the pleasure of transforming a mess. But also, as cleaning gigs went, the job was turning out to be fun. All day, Robert's friends and neighbors came and went performing chores which he'd concocted to keep them around: Morton took his shirts to the cleaner's; Alekande picked them up. Blair fed the fish. Blair had been in a car accident a few years before and couldn't bend his knees. In order to feed the fish, whose tank was near the ground, he got on the floor, did a pushup with one hand and shook the food in with the other. The mystery of the humans' food was solved when, at one, Alekande announced, "Who's hungry? I'm calling Beijing Palace."

On the other side of the wall from the tundra of the fridge stretched the oasis of the bar. This was the province of Vladimir who arrived with a brown paper bag containing a fresh supply of vodka. Ralph, the delivery boy from the liquor store, also showed up later that day.

As the only woman, I felt like Snow White among the seven dwarves. In the middle of the bustle Robert sat, Grumpy, perhaps, roaring, "Who's seen my yellow shirt? Alekande, have you got my yellow shirt? I told you not to take my yellow shirt."

"Why does Alekande put up with this?" I asked Morton.

"Why do any of us put up with it? Who do you think is paying off his college tuition loan? And mine? And Blair's physical therapy bills? At times, the quality of the food makes up for any drawbacks of the ambience. But basically, we're all Nevada whores, doing what we have to do to improve our lot in life. Has he asked you out to dinner yet?"

"No."

"He will."

I worked for two weekends wondering what these people, who constituted a family of sorts and who seemed bent on a career of hanging out, were doing with their lives. But I felt that I belonged there, at least for the time being. For I was not doing anything with my life that made sense to other people. I wrote but hadn't published anything. I was looking for a job teaching Music Theory but hadn't found one.

At six o'clock on Sunday of the second weekend, my dinner invitation came. It was time to go home – between housecleaning and waiting tables, I hadn't had a day off in two weeks – but I also hadn't been paid for the weekend yet. Robert saw my hesitation.

"Oh, come on," he said, "I've already made the reservation."

As Morton had implied, accompanying Robert to dinner was part of the deal.

He called a limo which took us to a restaurant in the east eighties that was so exclusive, I never learned its name. There was no sign outside. If you were walking by, you would just think it was another brownstone.

"The last time I was here," Robert said as we descended the steps, "was with Jackie O." I could almost believe this. Probably she'd been there having dinner with somebody else.

There was a pink rose on each table and the meal, which I don't remember except that it was exquisite, came to $200. This was vast, in those days. Robert, who'd been drinking since eleven and had ordered wine for both of us which he alone drank, didn't touch his food.

After dinner, we got back into the limo which was waiting outside.

"Central Park West, please," Robert said to the driver. I wanted to be paid and as Robert was too drunk to do anything violent, I didn't protest the instruction. At sixty-seventh street, his appetite returned so we stopped at Macdonald's where he had a hamburger.

As we entered Robert's building, his steps waxed and waned over the marble floor.

"Malcolm, you sonofawhoreson, I told you to send Emilio up yesterday. What happened?" he roared at the doorman, as though performing a satirical version of King Lear.

"Hello, Sweetness and Light," replied the doorman. "Malcolm will be here in the morning. I'll tell him you asked for him."

Apparently, this was a typical scene.

"I have to go," I said when we got upstairs. "I've got to get up for work tomorrow."

"I suppose that means you want your check," Robert returned.

I didn't say anything.

"Don't you have any manners?

'You can have your 'check,'" he continued, putting the word in scornful quotation marks as though to hold it at arm's length. "I'll give you a 'check' that's so large you'll be too embarrassed to cash it.

'But first, tell me about *muuusic*." He elongated the syllable with a musical lilt. It was ten thirty and I envisioned myself turning into Scheherazade for the long night ahead. I told him some stories from the backs of record jackets – the sort of anecdotes that appeal to people who feel more secure with human interest than with the abstraction of music: Albeniz was fat and never practiced; Rachmaninov died when a bookshelf fell on him.

"I thought composers all died of syphilis," Robert said, gearing up for an "intellectual" conversation. Getting out of there wasn't going to be easy.

"That was a hundred years ago."

"Who was the one who wrote dirty poems?"

"Mozart wrote dirty letters," I said wildly, hoping that would satisfy his yearning for dirt.

"Thank you," replied Robert with a dignity which, it seemed to me, the circumstances didn't merit.

He scrawled a check, dropping it at my feet as he passed on his way to the bedroom. Not too proud to pick it up, I looked at the amount: A hundred and forty dollars for the week-end. I was not embarrassed – on the contrary, I wondered if Robert was secretly sober, except that the next day, the bank officer had to call him to confirm the illegible signature.

The following Saturday after work, Robert took everyone out to dinner: Blair the fish-feeder, Blair's roommate, Josh; me, Tanya and Tanya's ex-husband, Jake. Jake was an ex-alcoholic and as we strolled back to Robert's apartment, he lectured Robert about the transformative powers of A.A.

"Fuck off," Robert replied in what was to prove to be one of the more civilized exchanges of the evening.

But Jake didn't fuck off. By the time we got upstairs (Blair and Josh having discreetly gone home) the two were shouting at each other, advancing and retreating in what might have appeared, to an onlooker in the building across the street, like a fencing match around the living-room.

"Help me with the leash," Tanya whispered harshly, taking advantage of the brouhaha to hustle Celine out of the apartment before Robert noticed.

I fumbled with the clasp and Tanya coaxed the uncertain dog through the door for her first walk in four years.

I hovered in the shadowy hallway, waiting for a chance to slip out after them. Then from somewhere – a desk drawer, probably, – Robert produced a gun. What I know for sure is that he stood waving it in the air, his body weaving over a coffee-table that had been hand-painted by an actress friend.

It was hard to take him seriously. But although Robert was full of hot air, it was possible the gun wasn't. I closed the front door softly behind me when a crash signaled that Robert had thrown the gun down, shattering the coffee-table.

Jake fled after me, panting, sweating, wide-eyed.

"Let's take the stairs," I said, knowing that in a moment Robert would follow.

We slipped through the service exit, Robert's voice

at the door of his apartment growing more faint as we ran down a flight and rang for the elevator. I hugged Jake, a way of hiding behind him, perhaps. His heart pounded like Robert's footsteps which I imagined pursuing us. (The following month, Jake would die of emphysema, diabetes and an enlarged heart.)

Outside the building, we ran into Tanya who, with the satisfied look of one who's achieved a long-awaited goal, was about to return the dog upstairs.

"I don't think that's such a great idea," I said and explained why.

The three of us took the dog to Tanya's house where Tanya and I slept in her double-bed and Jake slept on a convertible in the living-room.

All night the phone rang and with imperturbable patience, the machine took messages. The next morning we listened to them.

They were, of course, from Robert: "[*Unintelligible growling*]... lowest bunch of prissy, do-gooder ne'er-do-wellers I've ever had the misfortune to break bread with. [*Unintelligible.*] I should perhaps tell you that I called the police and you've been charged with kidnapping the dog."

Soon after, the police arrived and took down our version of the events of the night before. But they didn't seem interested and there was no follow-up. They did mention, however, that the gun had been loaded.

Remembrance of Things Passed and Failed

The first version of this article was written more than twenty years ago. I then sought permission from the Juilliard Public Relations department to publish it. They suggested dropping the matter if I wished ever to be allowed back in the building.

The article dove under the bed where it remained for the next several decades.

Juilliard has always had superb PR but it's of a glossy kind that was incompatible with the backhanded praise that the article offers. In fact, as a teacher, I was smitten with the school's brilliant students and faculty, its historic productions. Perhaps, if they ever get wind of the existence of this book and give a damn one way or the other, the current administration will understand that.

I fell in love with musical comedy at the age of five and with "concert music" (the pianist Rosalyn Tureck maintained correctly that the term "classical music" refers only to the late eighteenth century) at the age of thirteen. By the time I got to college, I wanted to teach what I loved.

That shouldn't have been too much to ask. But as everyone knows, to teach college (the level I wanted) you need a Ph.D. Much as I loved teaching, I hated being a student more. So I turned to Plan B. As there was no Plan B, I waited on tables.

In short order, I was fired from two positions: the first, for "allowing" a couple to skip out without paying their bill (for which I was illegally required to fork over my tips;) the second, for not being able to do that circus trick with plates up the arm.

So when a Fellowship opened up at Juilliard to teach Music History of the 19th and 20th centuries, I went through the motions of applying but forgot about the job as soon as I returned to my real life of getting nowhere. However, it was a few days before school was to open so only one other person had heard about the position. He was a better trained musician than I but with an expertise in a branch of theory considered too rarefied for undergraduates. He also had a thick Russian accent. I was hired.

Thrill soon gave way to terror. I'd gone to Juilliard for one misbegotten year of college and had been glad to be rid of the place. In those days, unlike today when the school is more open and humane, the core of the Juilliard experience lay in the practice room. In that sanctuary, nothing was supposed to come between the student, her instrument and the score. I had *wanted* things to come between us. The practice room was, for me, a vacuum. So I had left, gone to Hunter College and Oxford which offered more normal college experiences with conversation, other people, subjects beyond last night's performance of the Mozart 23rd Concerto.

But now I drew on that year at Juilliard for solace.

"They're not all ex-prodigies," I reminded myself. "And only a few are full-fledged virtuosi."

The reassurances rang pathetic. I envisioned lecturing to an audience that saw right through me to a core of incompetence.

But there was a core of energy too. I was twenty-five, not so long out of college myself, with the memory still dewy of boring classes which I'd fantasized about overhauling. My driving mission was to do unto my students as I wished had been done unto me. I might be ignorant but I would not be boring.

However, there was still the problem of preparing an hour and a quarter's class (to be repeated four times a week) for a whole year – the predicament of Scheherazade but without recourse to imagination. How to do this when I wasn't exactly brimming over with information?

"Keep them busy," I decided. "Exploit them: Get the singers to talk about opera," (the subject I knew the least about.) "They may resent it but at least they won't be bored. Or if they are, it'll be their own fault."

The Socratic method would be an indispensable tool in this process. Instead of imparting information, the teacher asks questions. Of course, you have to know where the conversation is going. Then again, maybe not. The ultimate goal of the Socratic method is for the students to ask their own questions while the teacher does nothing at all, disappearing like the Cheshire cat, with a grin.

Armed with a volume of Beethoven Sonatas, I greeted my first class with enough questions to fuel an hour and a quarter's discussion – I hoped.

"Was Beethoven a revolutionary?" I began.

It was 9.05 A.M. (Five minutes down to take attendance. Seventy minutes to go.) The class looked back blankly.

"Let's say, in the harmonies he used."

"Yeah, OK," the looks said. "Harmonies, whatever. So, tell us. Was he a revolutionary or not?"

"Well, let's see," I went on with mounting dread. "Open your scores to Opus 2 No. 2. What's the relationship between the key at the beginning of the movement and the key at the beginning of the development?"

Someone shifted in his chair. I looked sharply in the direction of the sound.

"Yes?"

But no, it had been just that – someone shifting in a chair. The class stared back like two rows of tombstones.

"Well, what is the key at the opening of the movement? Hello? Anybody home?" I felt like an explorer trying to humor his captors who don't speak the same language.

"A Major," a voice offered and it seemed indiscreet to try to identify it.

"Oh, I get it," somebody else said, "it's a mediant relationship?"

There is a God.

"Wait a second, isn't it supposed to be dominant?"

Pay dirt.

We were talking about the far-flung keys within the development when I asked for a volunteer to play the piece. The joyful noise of Youth at Work stopped. The pianists looked down at their shirt cuffs. ("Who, me? I play tuba.")

"Let's see... According to the registration cards...

Hei-Kyung Park, you're a pianist?"

"Yes."

"Would you like to try sight-reading this?"

"I have tendonitis."

"And who is... Robert Greene?"

A boy in the back row raised his left arm with a smile of faux regret: The arm was in a cast.

There was nothing for it but to read the work myself. I'd practiced for such an emergency. But one of the reasons I'd left Juilliard as a student was a small problem with paralyzing stage-fright. My hands shook or segued into alien keys as in a nightmare.

Performing in class now was hardly a gentle first step in overcoming this fear. Juilliard students are not known for their mercy.

As it turned out, though, my performance met with expansive pleasure; not of admiration but of relief. Never again did I have trouble getting volunteers to play. They knew the teacher was in no position to think harshly of their abilities.

The performances the kids did in class were among the high points of the year. Once I asked Joanna, an ultra-cool habitue of the cafeteria, to play the accompaniment to a Brahms lied.

She got up with as much enthusiasm as someone boarding the bus to go to work at the post office. Like a moody dryad, she wove her way through the thicket of desks to the piano, scanned the song she would be playing for the first time, and began.

Her instinctive sympathy for the music was apparent from the first phrase. The rest of us were aware we were witnessing something like the first meeting in what will become a love affair.

When we studied Schumann lieder and Michael D. sang part of a cycle, the songs fit perfectly in that setting of twenty people. The sense of drudgery that can sneak into classes vanished and the intimate audience transformed into a single organism, sensitive to every nuance.

But sometimes we talked about subjects which had nothing to do with scores, such as the art of the period we were studying. I couldn't elicit the students' ideas on the subject; they knew nothing about it. It was time to fork over hard information.

Students do not realize the extent to which their teachers suffer the syndrome commonly attributed to cockroaches: They are more afraid of you than you are of them. Although I boned up for these moments of truth, that wasn't the same as being a seasoned expert. Suppose someone asked a question? Still, my overriding fear remained that of being boring.

So I tried to deliver these mini-lectures with the eloquence which enthusiasm bestows. This approach backfired once when I spoke so fluently that after twenty minutes, I had nothing else to say. Fifty minutes remained to the class.

Several courses of action lay open:

1. Ask a general question – preferably one that can stir up fifty minutes' controversy.

2. Ask a difficult question for them to ponder while you think of your next move.

3. Repeat the lecture.

For the two years I taught classes at Juilliard, these insecurities never let up. But behind them lay another problem: that of ambition. I didn't want just to get through the year without disgrace; I wanted the students to take away knowledge they would use in their performances, pass on to their own students. What each person learned would be unique to him or her. It wouldn't be found in our textbook, stalwart and reputable as that was. They would learn it directly from the score which must be conceived anew by each musician who studies it as long as the music is to remain alive.

I also wanted to learn from my students, since that would be a sign I was doing the job right.

Occasionally, this happened. From one student paper, for instance, I learned that the professions of Rossini's parents had been those of trumpet player and slaughterhouse inspector. The paper didn't say which parent was which.

The most eye-opening observations came from students who knew the least for then they had to invent. Asked on an exam about Luisa Miller and The Sicilian Vespers, both operas by Verdi, a bassoon player described them as "friends of Liszt." (Along with La Somnambula and The Flying Dutchman?) Another question listed ten terms to be identified: Idee fixe, cyclic form, the sort of thing that comes up in Music 101 courses. A bonus term was "roller skates" which had been used to simulate ice skates in a Meyerbeer opera. Somebody cited them as an example of cyclic form. I gave her an extra point.

The students also had a certain stylistic flair, however inadvertent. In a paper on cello music of the Romantic era, one student said of the great composers who'd written solo works for the instrument, "These giants were largely responsible for the growth in the cello literature in the nineteenth century."

It's rare that one comes across such consistency of metaphor. How appropriate that giants had been responsible for growth and that the way they had been responsible was "largely."

Then there were the kids who by the end of the year came through, writing papers from the heart: the percussionist who wrote about Beethoven's Ninth and who is now himself on the percussion faculty of Juilliard; the pianist who ended a paper on Chopin's Nocturnes with the words, "It is impossible to imagine a world without them."

There were other redeeming features, too, to staying late, slogging through seventy-four essays on traditional form in Wozzeck: Dropping in on a play on the third floor; or simply hearing the pure tones of balanced winds filtering through the walls of a practice room.

One evening, I followed more distant sounds to their source two floors below the Music History office. Slipping in through the back door of the orchestra rehearsal hall, I stood inside for twenty minutes – a moment in which an impression was fixed in my mind of the palpable quality of a childhood memory – as the elegant gestures of Copland described in the air the phrases of Haydn.

Laura

Late one afternoon, wandering the hall at Juilliard, I bumped into F., one of the opera coaches.

"I'm going to Italian class," she announced proudly. "Want to come?"

I had nothing better to do so I went.

Laughter echoed down the hall from the classroom as F. and I approached. It was the last period of the day, ending at seven, so no one felt like working. It didn't matter; we fooled around in Italian.

Laura was a natural teacher. To illustrate the Italian word for "hide," she crouched in the corner; to demonstrate "argue," she launched into a heated dispute with an imaginary driver. Afterwards, the class went out to dinner at a nearby Italian restaurant where we ordered wine and laughed about our impossible lives.

I attended that class for two years but stayed in touch with Laura after that. Usually we met at the Metropolitan Museum for like many Italians, she loves art, going so far as to take up painting herself. She talked about her sons: One a lawyer, the other, in government.

She rarely spoke of her own past for she didn't like to be the protagonist of conversation. But one day she told this story:

In 1945, when she was seventeen, she joined an anti-Fascist group in Italy for which she was imprisoned for three months, only getting released because the Allies were near.

"Were you angry at your jailers?" I asked.

"No... I was too scared."

"What did they do to you?"

"Nothing. They left us alone. I was with a group of prostitutes. I learned such things!

'But you see, the body takes over. I shook for fourteen days from fever. By the end, I was delirious; I forgot who I was."

After the war, Laura and her husband – a German resistor who had been imprisoned first by the Nazis, then by the Russians – moved to America and had their first child.

One day about ten years later, Laura's brother knocked on the door and as a joke, announced he was the Gestapo. She began to shake again.

She has just seen Schindler's List.

"I have a clear sense of right and wrong," I said, "but if I'd been German or Italian in the early forties and against the war, I'm not sure I'd have had the courage to speak up."

"Yes, me too, now," she said. "When I hear something in the street like an argument, I leave quickly, eh? You have to, to survive in my neighborhood." (She lived on 122nd Street.) "But it's different with a group."

"If it happened again," I asked, "would you join the Resistance again?"

And she, vibrant painter, mother, teacher, lover of life, food, art... said, "I'd kill myself."

Why a Critic?

There comes a point in most people's lives, usually around the age of twenty-five, when they give up asking the big questions: "Who are we?" "How did we get here?" "Why do we exist?" Those sorts of questions. We shrug and get on with doing the laundry.

But some of us find it harder to get over asking those questions about a species several ranks above the human: that of the Critic. "Who is he?" and, "How did he get there?" are laments still heard in the wee hours at newsstands the length of the Upper West Side where the Critic's latest victims first encounter his unique form of assault.

It is in response to these anguished cries that I offer the following explanation:

First: Who is he? (Most often phrased, "Who is this guy, anyway?")

The Critic in our society is equivalent to the Brahmin in India. He is a more highly evolved form of ourselves, on a plane closer to God. His role in relation to the rest of mankind is as man's role in relation to the rest of nature. For just as we may pay lip service to the idea that dolphins have a language as complex as our own and a dolphin God; just as we may profess awe for the ants' social structure but at the same time take for granted that evolution leads up to us and that animals exist in order to serve us, or rather, be served to us as food, so does the Critic believe that art exists as meat into which to sink his fangs.

Second: How did he get there?

Like the Brahmin, the critic of a major newspaper got there through a series of progressive incarnations. Usually, he has come from a smaller, provincial newspaper in a Midwestern state and prior to that, an even smaller paper in a Midwestern town. This sheds additional light on the question of who or what he is for in fact, what he is and always has been is a Critic. A music critic, for instance, cannot afford to be too familiar with the processes of composition or performance. If he is, he will be considered biased.

Finally: Why do Critics exist?

The raison d'etre of the Critic is to represent the ideal audience, to be educated yet open, a fair judge of the fairness of the fare.

The road to this enlightenment is hard. At the opera one night, the Critic must know not only about voices and instruments but also about sets, languages and musical construction and maybe even black magic, passion and Freemasonry as well. The next night, he may be expected to have at his fingertips esoteric knowledge about ornamentation in the Renaissance and the night after that, about Tibetan chant or the square root of pi.

The Critic also seems to have been brought up with the maxim, Know Thyself, for this often serves as his final criterion. Like the average man to whom and for whom he supposedly speaks, (although the people who read reviews most avidly are the artists in them and their managers,) the critic may not know everything but he knows what he likes.

Then, with the idea of casting down the mighty and exalting the meek, he will deem a seasoned artist (one who has played for at least ten seasons) to be a mere pedant, damn a batch of reviews over here and give rhapsodic raves to one or two over there.

The next morning, the s*** hits the proverbial fan. For the Critic's power is vast. Over reams of paper and seas of ink his realm extends, through word of mouth, into the very air. Across the land, futile cries are heard to tear the heart and the hair. For in spite of our efforts to understand and assuage, the Critic is, finally, as inscrutable as the God whose power his approaches: It is not our place to fathom his mysterious ways.

Professor

The Contract Law professor was bear-sized. He had a Jewish name but as far as he knew was, with the exception of the Russian ancestor who had contributed the name, entirely Danish. He had lived in China and had earned an Oxford degree and a Doctorate from the University of Madrid at the same time. Both he completed with highest honors. The professor spoke the languages of all the afore-mentioned countries.

He felt that he was missing something. Students had written on teacher evaluations that he seemed indifferent; that during lectures, he didn't look at them. These criticisms bothered him as did his own lack of a stronger reaction but he still didn't look at them. His lectures were also marred by "er's" which were like knots in the otherwise golden thread of his speech.

A modern student would undoubtedly shrug off these eccentricities as the products of Asperger's but the professor had a different interpretation. He maintained, in a private conversation after class, that they stemmed from the torture he had endured in Korea. He spoke about this with no greater emotion than he spoke of Contract Law.

He also brought up other tragedies such as that of a well-known comedian whose 10-year-old son had had leukaemia. The boy did not realize the seriousness of his condition until a reporter asked him, "How does it feel to know you're dying?" When the professor told this story, we both laughed in astonishment. It was either that or cry.

The professor was leaving the school which had protested that his grades did not follow a curve. He had argued in response that the students' work had not followed a curve. His final gesture was to award everyone in the class some kind of B or A, thus proving himself more human than the students had given him credit for.

Roy Cohn

I went through law school in a fog of boredom, insecurity and resentment. On top of my lack of affinity for the subject, I detested legalese. A lawyer's job, it seemed, was to expound on everything from the drearily arcane to the painfully obvious.

But law school left a few indelible memories.

One night after Criminal Law class, Roy Cohn spoke.

The audience was sparse: By nine-thirty, most students – who worked day jobs in addition to attending school – had opted to go home.

I'd heard about Cohn, of course. He looked like the man who had been described. He was, as the saying goes, as ugly as sin. I was surprised; Hitler wasn't ugly. But Cohn looked like the portrait of Dorian Gray after it had been in the attic for a lifetime. I thought of Camus' warning that by fifty, one is responsible for one's own face.

In his introduction, the Criminal Law professor said that, with due reservations, he considered himself one of Cohn's friends. He also cautioned us not to ask Cohn about the Rosenbergs as Cohn had made that a condition of doing the lecture.

Thus the talk focused on his career as a criminal defense lawyer, about which it was unilluminating except in so far as it revealed Cohn's slimy philosophy: Everyone is out for himself so just learn to play the game. Cohn seemed to have no misgivings about this. He wasn't hypocritical so much as unabashedly corrupt.

In the question period that followed, I asked if, in his criminal defense work, he ever considered any ethical question besides how to win. He thought for a moment. Then, with a nonchalant shrug bordering on insolence, he said, "No."

The Seasons

When I look back, what looms largest, going on for the longest time, is not the recent past but the beginning. The rest recedes, foreshortened, as time accelerates to the vanishing point of now.

In the beginning, things were permanent. From birth to fourth grade was an infinite unity, an eternal Yin-Yang cycle of seasons.

First came tights season which began in October and lasted until April when Mum packed our winter woolens in white boxes, saved from Christmas, to be stored at the top of the closet. Down came the summer wardrobe: short socks which could be folded over or rolled down; sun-suits until I was four; gingham shorts sets in pink, blue or brown after that. I unfolded these outfits, surveying them with renewed pleasure, as with friends one only sees at camp.

Spring was leaves and sunlight; winter, a string of Christmas lights like stars. But the cycle itself would never change.

When I was ten, my father got a job in a theatrical agency with far-flung offices; we moved to London. All the seasons were rain and like everyone else under the age of thirteen, I wore knee socks for most of the year. Once there were snowflakes two days before the arrival of summer.

We lived in a block of "flats" that encircled a large, asymmetrical garden. In a dark, moist dugout behind the hedge, those in the vanguard of puberty revealed their burgeoning bodies which were fascinating in their pink bulges and folds. A boy with a teenage sister brought word to the rest of us about the changes that lay ahead.

The garden had its own cycle and rhythm: In winter, it was wood under a woolly grey sky; in summer, green and blue. But I, uprooted and transplanted, had acquired the third dimension of a past: I realized that the egg came before the chicken. What had laid the egg was not another chicken but a pre-chicken type of creature in the scheme of evolution.

The endless cycle of time broke – its two dimensions, an illusion. Looked at in three dimensions, it was a spiral going somewhere.

When I was fourteen, we moved back to New York. For the first time, I went to a private school. Gone were the days of bright summer clothes and colorful winter woolens. Year round, we schoolgirls wore a uniform the color of seaweed with an aqua shirt. We turned our backs on the outside world. What lay before us were books, fat ones containing hundreds of onionskin pages with inches of footnote debris at the bottom.

Friendship was not encouraged at this school for fear it would interfere with study. Looking 'round in alarm at the past, I saw that the garden gate, both real and metaphorical, had locked behind me. There was no going back.

From now on, the seasons were marked by exams, two sets of midterms, two sets of finals. No matter what the phase of the year, always somewhere in my mind was Exam week, a stretch of Judgment Days when we would be called to account for the previous two months. I saw all activities in terms of their payoff at exam time. Would I learn something from them? Were they diversions necessary for my sanity and hence, my ability to perform on the exams?

Walking alone in the park on weekends, or by the river when insomnia sent me to school at sunrise, I became aware of transience. The brown leaves of autumn began to fall in August and in February there were signs of spring. The cycle, transformed in England, had become more complicated.

What sustained me during those years were the piano lessons I took outside of school. My teacher, "Miss Laudon" in *To Everything There Is a Season*, imbued me with hope as Pygmalion breathed life into Galatea. Music was an island of love in a vast, ominous sea. As few others in my class at school were even interested in it, music became my island by default.

In college I continued to keep the world at arm's length, retreating to the island of music where Beethoven was the mountain range; Bach, the city; Schumann, the ocean; Chopin, the gardens. But this sojourn was transient too and I worried about how I would fit into the world when time, hurtling forth, dropped me there at graduation.

I wanted to teach Music Theory. I'd found hidden unity in Bach that I wanted to show anyone who would listen. But for that, you needed a Ph.D. While gathering the resolve to pursue one, after college I trained for a job, which everyone who heard about it professed to envy, supervising music at a soap opera.

The production half of the studio was a dark, sealed room smelling of old, cold cigarette smoke. There were no musicians to supervise, nor any instruments. The music came off tapes catalogued in the library as Neutral, Romantic or Tension. I was ashamed of the job, antsy spending time on something that required so little thought. It grew especially annoying when, after three months, Big Jack, the man I was supposed to replace when he retired, decided to stay on.

The seasons went underground. Or rather, I did. Each day at five o'clock, I walked my boss to his car in the garage across the street. Once the clocks moved back, it was dark when we left the studio. The garage was depressing and the smell, sickening. The future seemed like a tunnel without light at the end. Five months later I quit, after more training than is bestowed on an astronaut.

The following year I dreaded autumn.

Each year after that, the dread appeared earlier: first in June when the days began to get shorter; then in December as soon as they started to get longer again. This lasted until I read about light deprivation depression. Finding that other people suffered it too, I didn't get it again. By that time I was teaching Music History at Juilliard – a dream job although the meager pay necessitated moving back in with my mother. I taught fledgling pianists, singers, composers; lunched with established pianists, singers, composers.

The bus home passed through the park at sixty-fifth street. In December, the lights at Tavern on the Green outlined the bare-branched trees beneath which stood deer that appeared to be sculpted from ice. I wondered if the late December date had been chosen to celebrate Christ's birthday in order to get us through the darkest month.[6] Once again, winter was a string of Christmas lights like stars.

As adulthood continued, the seasons came in more intense and accelerated currents. By August, the street was strewn with dry brown leaves which strictly speaking, shouldn't have happened until November. And there was a silence in the city as though we were in the eye of the storm of time. I had more ill-fitting jobs that I couldn't wait for an excuse to leave. The desire for a child gestated in me but prospective fathers came and went, elusive as shadows.

I dreamed, also, of adult love. That dream was old. It had been born the first day of first grade when I fell under the spell of Miss Savoy, our sweet, clear-voiced teacher in the so-feminine full skirt of 1962. At twenty-eight, I had flashes of oneness during deep sex but they later proved to have come from my imagination which is to say, from hope.

Each season contained the seeds of the next, of the same season the following year and finally, of all future seasons. Anticipation took over awareness of the present and I saw transience everywhere: In a gurgling baby, I saw the sulking hulk of the adolescent. In a sparkling first meeting, I saw through to the banal middle of the relationship and its ugly end. I looked ahead not one season but five, thence straight to the end of my life. Time was pulling us towards the ultimate deadline like a vortex towards the center. I thought: *Life is a moment; then comes an eternity of memory. Surely there's more to it than that.*

Part Three:
The Kid

Newborn

In a coup, he has taken over our lives. His grandmother calls from the Bowery where she is scouring neighborhood thrift shops for a pram. His aunt returns from the supermarket with three phone numbers, torn from the noticeboard, of people selling baby furniture. His uncle mutters about the attention paid the new, unknown being.

In the eye of the storm he sleeps in sphinx position, his legs tucked under his backside.

What a piece of work is a baby. His feet, like sensitive plants, curl and unfurl at the touch as though shadow-boxing. Sitting up, he has the gravity of a statesman about to deliver an important pronouncement. The matter is resolved in a burp.

Since his birth, the rest of the world has receded. Russia and Europe are ciphers, as when one looks into a valley at the tiny houses far below. Nothing is so fascinating as the feathery down of his back; the ever-changing kaleidoscope of his expressions before his eyes slide away, back to sleep.

Chris

When Alex was a baby, each morning as I fed him, I turned on Sally Jessy Raphael. Raising a baby, particularly during the winter, can be an isolating experience; Sally was my conduit to the grown-up world. I looked forward to her show as I'd awaited Tuesdays at Juilliard when all the faculty were in attendance and ten of us gathered with our bag lunches around a table for four.

One morning, Sally had on a guest who was a hermaphrodite. The hermaphrodite had an androgynous name, which I will say was Chris, and androgynous clothing. I will call Chris "he" since one must decide on a pronoun and he seemed to me a little more he-ish than she-ish. Although twenty-seven, he had the voice and skin of a fourteen-year-old boy. But he would be offended at the pronoun as throughout the show he steadfastly maintained that he was no more one sex than the other.

Chris was oddly intriguing even apart from his unusual condition. He had a quirky philosophical attitude towards his status in the world and was earning a Master's degree in Psychology. I wondered what his thesis was on.

The audience seemed bent on pushing him towards a decision.

"But what do you fill out on bureaucratic forms?" one person wanted to know.

"Neuter," said Chris with the ease that was his disconcerting stock-in-trade.

"Have you had a chromosome test?" asked someone

else suspiciously.

They seemed to feel that Chris was claiming to be two people in one body and that that would lead to a stalemate, like a senate that voted 50/50.

"Yes," Chris answered. But he would not divulge the results of the test because, he said, what would it mean if a test said you had the genes for blue eyes when in fact you had no eyes at all?

As the show went to commercial Sally asked him, "Does God make mistakes?"

"I don't think He made a mistake with me," said Chris.

"I won't forget you," said Sally and she seemed to mean it.

After the show I wrote to Chris, telling him of Quentin Crisp, a transvestite in the days before homosexuality became the cause du jour. In his youth he had been beaten and persecuted but after garnering acclaim as a television wit, he had morphed into an icon to gays and straights alike. He maintained that by going on television, a person, in effect, washes away all his sins. It is as though one has regained one's virginity. This is the advice referred to in the title of his book, How to Become a Virgin.

Chris replied, "I was a virgin *before* I went on television."[7]

Gabriel's Story

*Be not confused, Reader. Despite appearances –
naïf style, crude drawings, child protagonist – this is not a
children's story. It's about a little kid but it's for parents,
grandparents, baby-sitters and anyone else who has had
anything to do with little kids.*

One night around two A.M., a woman woke up and
gasped, "Pigs' knuckles." Her husband grunted.

The woman explained: "I've got to get some pigs'
knuckles."

"Why?"

The woman got out of bed and began to get dressed.

"Have you ever had pigs' knuckles?" her husband
asked, a little more awake now.

"No. Go to sleep. I'll be back soon."

The woman went to an all-night deli where a thin,
balding man, who squinted as he emerged from a back
room, found her a jar of pigs' knuckles. Indeed, they hit the
spot.

This was the first sign of an event to come that would
change the couple's life forever.

Eight months later, on April 11th, Gabriel was born.

He was light as a bubble and did all the things babies are supposed to do.

When he was two months old, his mother took him for a walk.

"That's a grocery store," she said. "That's a tree… That's a doggie."

Gabriel took in these wonders like someone who is in the process of waking up.

The world was of absorbing interest but didn't come as a surprise. He'd grown accustomed to its sounds while he napped and to its sights while he fed. Now began the task of figuring it all out.

As it happens, the household into which Gabriel had been born was a little weird.

For one thing, Mamma recycled plastic containers until they cracked. At first, she relabeled the containers. But when there got to be too many labels, she just refilled the containers and left them in the freezer. So Daddy had become used to opening yogurt cartons that had last been labeled "Chicken Soup" and finding chocolate pudding inside.

Also, because the kitchen was visited by roaches at night, Mamma had developed another idiosyncrasy. If she had a snack after she'd gotten ready for bed, then rather than go outside to throw away the garbage, she wrapped it up and put it in the refrigerator til morning. This practice troubled Daddy who periodically organized the refrigerator along evolutionary lines with manmade foods on the top shelf.

One night as Mamma was carrying a sleeping Gabriel to his room, he woke up, realized where they were going and cried.

"Come on, Gabriel," Mamma soothed him. "It's time to go to bed. Mommy and Daddy are tired."

Gabriel cried more loudly. He wasn't tired. He was, by now, fully awake and fighting for his rights.

"Do you want some oatmeal?"

Gabriel stopped crying.

Mamma carried him into the kitchen and poured some oatmeal into the bowl with a scene from Beatrix Potter painted in the middle. Gabriel ate half the cereal. The other half ended up on his nightshirt. To elude the roaches, Mamma changed Gabriel's nightshirt, putting the dirty one in the refrigerator.

The next morning, when he reached in for the milk, Daddy found it.

"Mmm!" he said in mock appreciation. "With a little bearnaise sauce, this'll be delicious. Label it 'Peanut Butter.'"

In an effort to introduce a little more normality into their household, one day Daddy invited Gabriel's uncles, Scott and Alan, to come over. Scott was an accountant and Alan, a systems analyst. You couldn't ask for a more normal pair of uncles.

After an hour of sitting around talking and snacking on a bag of bagels they'd picked up at the 7-11, Scott and Alan babysat while Mamma went shopping.

When she came back, she found them at opposite ends of the hall sending the carriage back and forth. Inside, Gabriel was propped up like an alert dog, watching the world whiz past.

"Oh dear," sighed Mamma, putting down her shopping bags. "I'd so hoped you'd teach him how to be normal."

"I brought some sample 1040's," said Scott. "And Alan brought 'Javascript 101.' This whizzing business was his idea." He shrugged in Gabriel's direction.

"Perhaps we should give it a little more time," Mamma said. "Stay for dinner."

At dinner, Gabriel eschewed the meal the others were having of Boeuf Bourgignon with a delicately balanced Merlot, opting instead for applesauce à la Gerber and eight ounces of milk.

But afterwards, he sat on Scott's lap ("like a leprechaun perched on a mushroom," Mamma thought fondly,) and stared at his uncle's breast pocket, all the while listening with apparent interest to the discussion of recent changes in the tax law.

"All right, Gabriel," Mamma sang when Alan rose to leave. "Time to go to bed." And she reached for her baby. Gabriel reached up too. In his fist were a twisted Kleenex and a crumpled one dollar bill.

"Where'd he get those?" asked Mamma in wonder. She lifted Gabriel off Scott's lap. A pile of pennies fell to the floor, rolling under the china cupboard.

"That stuff?" said Scott. "That's mine." He looked in his jacket. "He's been picking my pocket."

"Hmm," thought Mamma, her brow furrowing, "Maybe there really was something to that rumor about Mom and Harpo Marx."

For a while it looked as though she was onto something since Gabriel was turning into a deft pilferer. Normal, schnormal… he just wanted to know what was inside things. Usually he concentrated on dirty laundry but sometimes his taste was more alarming. While Mamma talked to Midge next door, he riffled her handbag for a juicy leather wallet which he chewed for the rest of their conversation.

The other clue that Gabriel might be a descendant of Harpo was that wherever he went, things fell off him, usually Koco Krispies. Koco Krispies turned up in the most unlikely places:

At three, Gabriel started helping Mamma around the house.

While she did chores, he worked alongside her, wiping the cabinets – at least, the parts he could reach – and helping her put away the groceries.

Then Mamma made a thick pea soup and baked a cake while Gabriel vacuumed.

"Good boy, Gabriel," said Mamma absently as she wondered where the flour had disappeared to and whether she was really going out of her mind this time.

"Now," said Mamma, "it's time to set the table for dinner. Watch carefully because you're going to do it all by yourself. See how I put the fork here and the knife and spoon on this side? Now you do exactly what I did but over here, in Daddy's place." And she left Gabriel alone to finish the job.

Gabriel approached it with all his three-year-old integrity, doing exactly what Mamma had said: He took the place setting that she had created and moved it, piece by piece, to Daddy's place.

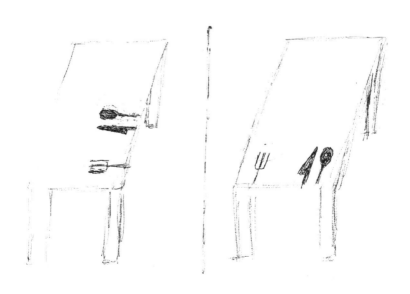

146

Daddy, who was fond of talking about "the big picture," focused on his son's new accomplishments. All right, so he still had an unusual hankering for milk as well as a habit of petty theft. And it was true that conversations with him often ended up far from where Daddy had thought they were heading. Still, he was showing a seriousness of purpose that needed to be fostered. It was time, Daddy decided, to show him how the world worked.

"Get ready, Gabriel," he said as he finished his breakfast soon after reaching this decision. "We're going to the plant."

"I'm thirsty," said Gabriel.

"Well, ask Mamma for some milk." Daddy suppressed a sigh of exasperation.

Mamma gave Gabriel some milk. Gabriel finished it.

"I want some more," he said.

Mamma poured more. Gabriel spilled it. Daddy looked at the ceiling while tapping his feet in a syncopated rhythm. Mamma refilled Gabriel's glass and took him to his room to change his shirt. On the way, Gabriel slipped on the spilled milk and got his pants wet. Daddy drummed his fingers on the kitchen table in counterpoint to his feet.

But finally, thirst quenched, tears dried and clothes changed, they were off.

"I learned this business from my dad," said Daddy as they strode towards the subway station, "and now I'm going to teach it to you."

"Who's your dad?" asked Gabriel.

"My dad was Harold Upright the Second."

"But Harold's deaf."

"Not deaf, Gabriel – dead."

Gabriel thought for a moment: "He's not dead; he's Dad."

Daddy changed the subject.

"The plant where we're going today, where Daddy works? It's the biggest plant in the Southeast," he told Gabriel proudly.

"Bigger than the lemon tree?" asked Gabriel since that was the biggest plant at his house.

Daddy laughed. "Bigger than a whole orchard of lemon trees. We make furniture for offices in Maryland, Delaware, the Carolinas... you name it. Won't that be fun?"

"Yes!" said Gabriel, staring into a toy store they were at that moment striding by. In the window, a diorama displayed a primeval swamp in which a Tyrannosaurus Rex stalked, her craggy mouth open in a roar. Behind her lay a broken egg with something wonderful inside: a baby dinosaur!

"Look, Daddy!" cried Gabriel. "Can we go in and pet the dinosaur?"

"Not right now, Gabriel. Listen!"

They were at the edge of an Arab neighborhood and a far-away man wailed to the sky. Daddy had not forgotten his pledge to show Gabriel how the world worked and what had just arrived was what teacher-training manuals call "a teachable moment."

"You see, Gabriel," Daddy said, "some people pray

to Allah and some people pray to God."

"They pray to Alan and Scott?"

"Yup. Come on; we have to get some money."

At the money machine, Daddy showed Gabriel what buttons to press. But somehow they ended up doing the transaction in Chinese.

Indeed, Gabriel saw when they arrived at the Plant, it was very big: It stretched from one horizon to the other.

"Would you look at that," sighed Daddy. "All those chimneys, Gabriel, are engines of productivity, industry... the economic health of this country."

He turned to Gabriel, expecting to see on the child's face the awe of taking it all in but Gabriel's eyes were fixed on the ground. He had found a creature that lived on the Plant: a fuzzy, grey caterpillar. Gabriel picked it up. The caterpillar looked around as though to say, "Hey, what's going on?"

"His name's Charlie," said Gabriel. "Do you want to hold him? He's not heavy."

"No, thanks," said Daddy impatiently. "Let's just take Charlie over to this patch of grass so he can build himself a cocoon and turn into a butterfly."

That sounded wonderful: The caterpillar could do magic! Gently, Gabriel put down the fabulous creature who lost no time before arching his way through the grass. He seemed to know where he was going.

"Come on, Gabriel," said Daddy. "We have to check on the generator."

They went to the main building and through a metal door that echoed after it slammed shut. In a room by itself, the generator shook with a deafening din.

"Ah!" said Daddy, "the heart of the whole operation. Fine, fine..."

After the generator, Daddy showed Gabriel the stock room, the loading dock and the offices.

"Will you take me here again?" Gabriel asked, his eyes shining, at the end of the visit.

"Sure," laughed Daddy, adding to himself, "I knew that under the right conditions, the child would come to his senses."

"So," said Mamma as she tucked Gabriel in that night, "I hear you had such a good time at the plant, you want to go back!"

"Yes!" Gabriel said, "I want to visit Charlie when he turns into a butterfly."

"Ah!" said Mamma with a rueful smile. "I thought it might be something like that... Good night, Kitten." And she bent down to give Gabriel a kiss.

"Good night, Mamma," Gabriel said.

Turning off the light as she went, Mamma tiptoed out.

From his bed Gabriel looked up into the outer space of the ceiling and prayed: *Dear Uncle Alan and Uncle Scott, for my birthday please could I have a real dinosaur egg with a baby dinosaur inside.*

After his trip to the Plant, Gabriel's curiosity became more focused. He still wanted to see what was inside things, same as before, but what he most wanted to see the inside of was eggs. At breakfast, he stopped drinking his hot chocolate in order to watch Daddy tap the crown of his soft-boiled egg before slicing it off and scooping up the yellow blood that trickled out. And he even agreed to eat quiche so Mamma would let him help her break the eggs to make it.

For ever since the day Daddy had taken him to the Plant, Gabriel had been on a mission. His curiosity had become charged with a longing to find in some dark hole, some as yet uncracked egg, that treasure, that missing link, that Holy Grail of his young life, a baby dinosaur.

It was taking a long time but meanwhile, his usual curiosity ensured that the world remained a fascinating place.

One night as Daddy and Mamma got ready for bed, they heard a noise outside their bedroom door: A rustling; the sound of light metal parts brushing past each other, then tense silence. A moment later, the patting of small feet running away down the carpeted hallway.

Mamma went to investigate but Gabriel lay in his bed, asleep.

The next night, the same hushed rustling started outside their bedroom.

Steeling himself to face the grim truth that he so dreaded, Daddy went to the door.

When Gabriel moved aside the metal sheath and placed his eye at the keyhole, he met a large, familiar eye looking back.

The door opened.

"Gabriel," said Daddy who was wearing a serious expression. "Did you ever hear the saying, 'Curiosity killed the cat?'"

Wordlessly, Gabriel shook his head.

"Well go to bed and think about it."

Gabriel went to bed and wondered who had killed the cat for being curious.

Meanwhile in the Uprights' bedroom Daddy, too, was troubled.

Why couldn't Gabriel be like little Tommy Trendsetter next door? he wondered as he paced back and forth in front of the bookcase. *He* didn't get mesmerized watching someone eat an egg. Tom Sr. said that every day after school, little Tom sat in front of the computer until dinner and after dinner too, until it was time for bed.

"It's my fault," Daddy said to himself as he glanced up at the T.V. show Mamma was watching in which a superhero called Telemarketing Man was saving the world from a deluge of schmalz.

Daddy continued to pace, head bowed to the floor which held no answers. Looking up in frustration he scanned the bookshelf absently when his eye lit on a title in bold black capitals: *Keeping Your Child on the Straight and Narrow*. With a skepticism that was intended to fend off disappointment, he leafed through it, pausing at the chapter entitled *Curiosity*:

There may come a time when despite all precautions, the child shows an interest in taboo subjects: Bugs, worms, his own body are a few examples of the discoveries children make at this stage which typically occurs between the ages of two and twenty-five. Children may also exhibit an

153

unseemly curiosity about matters that are none of their concern. This can cause anguish and embarrassment to parents who have done nothing to deserve such distress.

Should your child show such an inclination, nip it in the bud. Take a stand! Remove the offending stimulus to save your child from being lured into a world that is both strange and all too natural.

Thoughtfully, Daddy closed the book and slipped it back onto the shelf. He would take matters into his own no-nonsense hands.

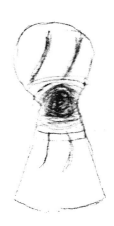

"What would you like to play?" asked Mamma the following evening after she and Gabriel had finished work for the day.

"Hide and Seek," said Gabriel.

"Why do I even ask?" muttered Mamma to herself. "All right. You go hide and I'll count." And she put her head down on her forearm. "One, two, three..."

Gabriel ran to hide in his favorite place, the hall closet, among the winter coats. But when he reached the dining-room, he stopped. Hide and Seek flew from his mind as Gabriel beheld the most wondrous sight he'd ever seen.

For there, next to the table, light, green and ready to spring, was a baby dinosaur. It had tiny scales, a curvy tail and a belly that expanded and contracted like the bellows when Daddy made a fire in the fireplace.

"Look, Mamma!" Gabriel cried.

The dinosaur darted its head to the left, changed position with lightning speed and froze once more, looking at Gabriel.

"Oh God," said Mamma when she came in, for what Gabriel had discovered was a lizard.

The lizard didn't move.

"What do I – ? What do we have – ? How – ?"

Looking in vain for something with which to get rid of the beast, Mamma picked up some pieces of Lego that were lying on the floor – glad, for once, to have them around – and one by one, threw them at the lizard.

That looked like fun – playing Dodgeball with the

baby dinosaur! Gabriel picked up other pieces and threw them also.

Under this rain of Lego the lizard stood, frozen.

Mamma and Gabriel picked up the pieces and threw them again. Finally, Mamma threw a wheel that hit the lizard which darted an inch. It looked different; could it be... shorter?

"I cut off its tail!" Mamma wailed, a little ill.

As the curtailed lizard ran around in circles, Mamma thought, with a sickly hope, "Maybe it's in some kind of pre-death dementia like a chicken without its head."

Then the tail, too, began to hop about.

"Aagh!" screamed Mamma and following the lizard and its tail, ran around in circles.

"What is going on?" asked Daddy who'd been working in his office upstairs. "Oh Jesus." At the sight of the crazed trio – Mamma, lizard, tail – chasing each other around, he groaned.

Without another word, Daddy acted to remove the offending stimulus. Heading stealthily towards the stereo where under the cliff of the speaker the lizard now crouched, its belly expanding and contracting, Daddy scooped up the lizard in one hand, marched over to the patio door, opened it wide and disappeared into the garden, returning a moment later, wiping his empty hands.

Gabriel watched, too paralyzed with sorrow to cry.

Without a backwards glance, Daddy marched up the stairs again to his office, closing the door with a decisive click.

In the newly silent dining room, Mamma looked at Gabriel.

"I'm sorry..." she said, tentatively.

Gabriel said nothing. He just stared at the place where the baby dinosaur had so recently and radiantly stood in the Uprights' very own dining-room.

"Would you like some milk?"

Gabriel shook his head.

"Do you want me to swing you around like a roller coaster?"

Gabriel shook his head again.

Mamma went over and put her arm gently around Gabriel's waist. Gabriel didn't move. He didn't cry or bury his head on Mamma's shoulder the way he usually did or put his arms around her neck so she would pick him up. He just stood still, his belly expanding and contracting like the bellows when Daddy made a fire in the fireplace.

When Daddy came home from work the next day, he went, as was his custom, to the garden to greet Gabriel.

Gabriel wasn't there.

"Gabriel?" called Daddy, puzzled.

"Yes?" answered Gabriel from within the house.

Daddy went inside.

"What did you do today? Did you make a house for your Lego people in my shoe?"

"No."

"Why not?"

"Lego people are toys. They're not real."

"Oh. Well I guess you're right... Did you play Hide and Seek with Mamma?"

"No."

"Oh. Why not?"

"She always knows where I am. She just pretends she doesn't... May I be excused now?"

"Sure, Son. You can be excused."

Puzzled, Daddy watched Gabriel go into the living-room.

"Probably going to turn on his favorite show, that's what it is," he said to himself.

Instead, Gabriel took the prospectus from the Plant that Daddy always left out on the coffee table for visitors and with a somber expression, turned its pages, looking at the pictures.

"What happened to our boy?" Daddy asked Mamma as they lay in bed that night, unable to fall asleep. "He seems to have grown up all of a sudden."

"Yes," said Mamma, sadly.

"I mean, I'm not complaining. The house is a lot neater now. And I sure don't miss finding alien objects in my shoes." Daddy gave a little shot of a laugh.

"Still..." said Daddy.

"Still..." echoed Mamma.

And with that, the Uprights lapsed into separate silences on their separate sides of the bed, each remembering the scenes he or she didn't miss.

"Want to play Pirates?" Daddy asked with unaccustomed enthusiasm the next night when he came home from a particularly long and demanding day.

"No, thank you," Gabriel said with what psychiatrists call a lack of Affekt.

"Want some Koko Krispies?" Mamma asked, having read that in times of stress, children may revert to an earlier phase. "A cookie?" And finally, in a desperate reach back to infancy, "Oatmeal?"

"No, it's O.K."

The Upright parents looked at each other, troubled, but at a loss about what to do since what they were confronted with was exactly what they'd always wished for.

One morning in April, Daddy was walking down the street in the wistful state that had become his habitual mood recently, when he passed the toy store where Gabriel had first seen the dinosaur display.

The scene in the window now was based on the theme of Easter. Rabbits cavorted in the grass with lambs and other young animals. And just as the dinosaur scene had featured an egg of wondrous content, this scene also featured eggs: Lots of them, in a broad spectrum of colors.

Daddy gazed for a while, lost in thought. Then, for the first time in many months, he grinned.

"Gabriel, get dressed," he said the following Saturday. "We're going out."

"O.K.," said Gabriel and without request or complaint, without slipping or any other mishap, he was ready in a few minutes.

Daddy took Gabriel's hand and walked him to the corner where they usually turned right to go to work or the bank or the subway. But now they turned the other way. Where were they going? Gabriel wondered but not intensely as it didn't matter. These days Gabriel went along with whatever his parents asked of him, without question.

They walked a few blocks, Daddy humming softly which was unusual. But Gabriel didn't think about it. What difference did it make whether Daddy hummed or not?

"See that block of offices?" Daddy asked, pointing at a squat, dark grey building across the street and down a few doors.

"Yes."

"That's where we're going."

Why was Daddy taking Gabriel there with a hint of a smile Gabriel had never seen him wear before?

The building was ugly with a strange name embossed in gold above the door: B.U.G. (Gabriel had begun learning his letters and "bug" was the first "B" word he could spell.)

"Broadway Union Gas," said Daddy.

In the window before them lay a pool of water with several dozen eggs resting along the rim in haphazard array.

Gabriel looked questioningly at his father. *So what?* the look said. *What's so special about eggs?*

"Watch!" whispered Daddy as though the eggs might hear him. "That one over there."

He pointed at an egg in the corner on whose shell a small hole had appeared. From the hole grew a crack. *Pause...* As though from the egg's own private earthquake, the crack extended at its lower end.

Gabriel stared. Something invisible was breaking the egg.

A small yellow triangle like a tiny chiseling tool poked at the egg shell from the inside.

Poke, poke. The egg was splitting. Inside, something moved around.

"Look, Gabriel! There's another one!" Daddy pointed excitedly at an egg on the other side of the pool.

That egg, too, had a hole in the shell which was being poked and pecked from the inside.

"Look!"

In the first egg, a craggy door had opened. A moist

head appeared, straining its way through. Then out of the shell fell a sticky, matted baby duck.

The duck righted himself, flapped, waddled to the side of the pool, flopped and went to sleep.

Now the second duck popped out of its shell, a little darker than the first. It, too, flapped its wings, stumbled and waddled over to the first duck, falling asleep against his back.

One by one, the shells cracked and ducks worked their way out. After five ducks had hatched and fallen asleep in a mound of fine yellow feathers, the first-born duck roused himself from his sleep, dry and fluffy, and flapped into the pool for a swim.

Gabriel watched without moving. With the same rapt attention, Daddy watched his son and the ducks in turn. In this way, father and son stayed at the Broadway Union Gas window until four o'clock when the duck-keeper arrived with a cardboard box, swept the newborn ducks into it – flapping and tumbling over each other – and took them home for the night.

"Did you like that, Gabriel?" Daddy asked as they walked back to *their* home.

Gabriel nodded with a secret smile Daddy hadn't seen in months. Daddy sighed in relief. Then he said, "The lizard would have escaped back to the garden anyway; you know that, don't you?"

Gabriel nodded again.

"Happy Easter."

Shaking a coffee cup, a homeless man bowed as Daddy and Gabriel passed. Daddy paused, fished a dollar out of his pocket and stuffed it in the cup.

"Alleluia," he said, under his breath.

A few weeks later when Gabriel went to bed, Mamma and Daddy came in to say good-night together.

"Gabriel," said Daddy. "Mamma and I have something to tell you.

'Mamma's going to have another baby."

"Tomorrow?"

"No; in about seven months."

"How long is that?"

"It's after Halloween."

"Where's the baby?"

"In Mamma's tummy."

Gabriel looked at Mamma's tummy.

"Is it an egg?"

Daddy winced but pulled himself together. "Mmm... sort of," he said.

Over the next seven months, Mamma's stomach grew fatter like the vacuum cleaner bag when it was full. When Mamma lay on her back, her stomach moved like thick pea soup coming to a boil.

Then one morning when Gabriel got up, instead of Mamma, he found Uncle Alan in the kitchen making him breakfast.

"Mamma went to the hospital this morning," he said.

"You have a baby brother – Gary."

Gary was soft and light like Charlie. Gabriel fed him milk and oatmeal. Later, he taught him how to vacuum and how to set the table for four people rather than one person in four places.

"He's not a baby dinosaur," thought Gabriel, "but he's better at soccer."

As for Mamma and Daddy, they looked at Gabriel and said, "He'll be an accountant yet, and a happy one. But the days of thinking everything has something magic inside seem to be over for good."

Then one day, it was Gabriel's turn to bring something to school for Show and Tell. He chose an oil lamp that Mamma had bought at a Middle Eastern store a few blocks away.

"How was your Show and Tell?" asked Mamma when she picked Gabriel up from school that afternoon.

"Good. But Mamma?"

"Yes?"

"I said something that might be a lie."

"What did you say?"

"I said it was made of gold. Is that O.K., Mamma?"

"Well, I guess it's O.K. So your report was a little less like journalism, a little more like fiction."

Gabriel sighed with relief.

"What else did you tell them about the lamp?"

"Oh..." he replied happily, "I told them there was a real genie in it."

Memoir of a Kawaggi* in Saudi Arabia

* Westerner

Eighteen years ago our family moved to Jeddah, Saudi Arabia, where my husband, Nick, had been sent by his maritime law firm. [Names have been changed and, for the record, the marriage, ended.] With last year's bombing of a compound like the one we lived on and with the probable inclusion of women in the Kingdom's next municipal elections, it seems time to reflect on a lifestyle that's gone the way of the ha-ha plant.

"A maritime law firm in the desert?" exclaimed the pianist Rosalyn Tureck when I told her where we were going.

But Jeddah is a port and anyway, Nick's firm was expanding to include international law.

I didn't want to move to Saudi Arabia. There'd just been a spate of hijackings and even if we got past the improbable hurdle of being blown up on the way over, I worried that a truck could barrel past the compound guard with a bomb aboard.

"Nothing like that has ever happened," Nick said reassuringly. *[Addendum 2012: It happened fourteen years after we left, in 2003 and again in 2009.]*[8] "Saudi Arabia isn't like the rest of the Middle East. It's a repressive regime; no one dares even steal your pocketbook; they'd get their hand cut off."

Ah, the upside of repression... I called a former CIA

agent who'd been on the radio after writing a book about the Kingdom.

"If you hear of any trouble – unrest among foreign workers, for instance – you should leave," he advised. He knew that all was not well in the state of that Shangri-La we were moving to.

Then the hijackings stopped so I agreed to go.

I bought a book to learn Arabic. It was uphill work. For one letter of the alphabet the book recommended, "Approximate the sound one makes when blowing on one's glasses." Transliterations were crude: I showed a certain word, written in Roman letters but translated three unrelated ways on the same page, to an Egyptian friend. She frowned and said, "I do not know this word. Why are you studying Arabic? Everyone you'll meet will speak English."

"I figure if we get taken hostage, they might look more kindly on the family of someone who knows a bit of the language."

"They'll think you're a spy."

Jeddah airport: Gleamingly modern but for the black ghosts mingling with the bustling crowd. Dressed like medieval executioners, they were largely silent. So it was disconcerting when one of them yelled, gesticulating that I was standing on the wrong line.

We moved to a compound I shall call the Garden of Jeddah. Like an imaginary island I dreamed up when I was eleven, it had one of everything: One grocery store where if some product a resident desired was missing, the eager-to-please Filipino manager ordered it from the supermarket; one restaurant; one dry cleaner; one doctor. If the air conditioner acted up or failed to, if the sink got clogged, the compound sent over a Filipino worker to fix it, no charge.

"Filipinos fix everything," grinned a maintenance worker as he tinkered with the T.V. These days they probably fix computers too.

People ask if it took a long time to get used to life in Saudi Arabia. It took two days. After being shown around Jeddah by Laurie, the wife of the head partner at the firm, (shopping malls downtown; a lovely Old Section with delicately wrought, though not particularly sturdy, wooden balconies,) every day was the same: Writing in the morning while our son was at preschool; childrearing for the rest of the day. Some women complained about not being allowed to drive. I wondered where they wanted to go. With its gardens and turquoise-tiled fountains, the oasis of the compound approached one's deep-rooted notions of Paradise, lending plausibility to the local legend that Eve was buried nearby.

The lifestyle of luxurious house arrest suited my introspective tendencies at the time. But when I ventured outside preoccupations with my book or my family and focused on the world we lived in now, it presented a disheartening picture. Garden of Jeddah was Pleasantville, the women wafting inexorably toward Stepford wifehood.

The noticeboard at the compound's Information Center was gaily bursting with announcements of classes in everything from quilting to crocheting; from flower arranging to cake-decorating – enough activities to gain the place instant accreditation as a lunatic asylum. "It helps to have an engrossing hobby," Laurie advised. One woman worked all winter on a really big jigsaw puzzle.

You might think that in such an environment, where we were thrown together as on an episode of Survivor, gossip and intrigue would flourish. No such luck. Conversation around the pool dwelt mainly on vacations and beauty aids. In the two years we were in Jeddah, I heard of only one affair and of that, only that the new couple were unhappy. There were three pool drownings of children too, one of them on our compound: A five-year-old Sudanese boy, the son of one of the maids. "He used to chase the ball when we played tennis," a neighbor reflected. The company that employed the maid paid for her to fly home to bury her son. A week later, she returned to work. No safety gates were put up around the pools. Life went on as though nothing had happened.

No one talked about the news either, not that there was much to talk about. The local papers consisted of a couple of pages of international news and one page devoted to Saudi achievements, most frequently in the Medical Column which might have been better described as the Kidney Transplant Column. The most entertaining section of the paper contained reports from uncertain sources of events such as the birth to a family in rural China of a twenty-third child; like all the other children, a girl.

The news wasn't censored so long as reports covered approved topics and with a positive spin. "No news is bad news," seemed to be the motto, "unless it's taking place somewhere else." Emily, a journalist friend, said she was even told to write upbeat restaurant reviews.

The weather was censored too. Newspapers downplayed the temperature – as measured on several people's home thermometers – when it went above fifty degrees Celsius since at that point a work stoppage would have to be declared for outdoor labor.[9] Although when the temperature once hit 53 degrees Celsius (127 degrees Fahrenheit) no one bothered to conceal the truth; you knew it as soon as you touched the handle to the car door.

Foreign magazines that didn't toe the line got the full treatment: References to pork, alcohol, nudity and any religion other than Islam were censored with a scribble of black magic marker. The practice added a whole new dimension to crossword puzzles. Sometimes ads were ripped out entirely so that you also lost the news on the other side of the page.

One night we watched a movie in which several women sat around a pool in bathing suits. A black block covered each one like a literal body guard, bobbing along in front of her when she got up to stroll languidly to the house. Once the censor got distracted; the black block lagged behind the woman so we got a glimpse of the forbidden bod until the block caught up.

There was a wedding in that movie too but since it took place in a church, we never found out what happened.

T.V. news consisted largely of events such as graduations presented in toto. So we savored the Today

Show, although the seventeen hour time lag in airing overseas prompted one compound wag to dub it the Yesterday Show.

Real news travelled through the grapevine. This was how we learned of a change in the law that was to affect Nick's client, Michael: Henceforth, imported barley was to be dyed red to distinguish it from the local variety and thereby protect the market. The authorities had released a recipe for dyeing the barley which Michael said resembled his grandmother's method of dyeing Easter eggs. The law was effective immediately. Michael had two tons of barley due to arrive the following Monday.

Even the beauty itself of Garden of Jeddah was unnatural. Thanks to the regular "fogging," in which a worker came by on a mini-tractor from which billowed clouds of pesticide, we never had so much as a fly. The compound management downplayed any ill effects to humans of the chemical formula behind this miracle but when several residents developed neurological symptoms, they were found to have elevated levels of arsenic in their blood.

However, not even the powerful brew that staved off insects, vermin and birds could completely prevent a phenomenon during our second year: The sky grew yellow and the next morning, the trees were bare while dead locusts dotted the garden paths.

And what, people ask, was it like to be a woman in Saudi Arabia?

A neighbor who ventured downtown during a

religious holiday got hassled for not wearing a scarf. The mutawwa (religious policeman) was stunned when she turned around for unlike her big blond hair, her face did not conceal her seventy years. When they deemed your skirt too short, she said, they hit your legs with a stick.

My own encounter with Arab antifeminism took place one afternoon when a teenager, rampaging along the garden paths on a motorcycle, came within a foot of my two-year-old son. The compound management refused to act; I called the police.

"Your husband has to make the report," they said.

"He's not here; he didn't see the incident. He doesn't know anything about it."

"Your husband has to make the report."

Then there was the quaint (and by now obsolete?) criterion for testifying in court, relayed to us by a reputed scholar of Shari'a law: The testimony of two women is equal to that of one man. But most weighty of all is the testimony of an adult male Muslim who has never urinated standing up; a criterion that would, of course, be easily satisfied by an adult female Muslim or male Muslim baby.[10]

More insidious than the overt misogyny of the Arabs was the patronizing attitude of our Midwestern compatriots, asking Nick about his "better half" and refusing to call me by my own last name. It was easier with Saudis according to whose custom, we were told, women are not considered worthy of taking their husband's name.

As for the attitude that women tempt men through their dress to commit rape, it wasn't so different from the excuses one sometimes hears in this country.

"Guess what!" announced a man at a cocktail party at the Consulate. "The X Company won their fight with the Saudis. Remember how they wanted to use female secretaries but the Saudis wouldn't let them? Well, the Saudis backed down! The women secretaries can come over!"

"All right!" Everyone raised their glasses. "Yes!"

I exchanged glances with Emily, the journalist. Did insisting on female secretaries now pass for feminism? It was sometimes hard in Saudi Arabia to know whose side to be on.

The other response people have to hearing we used to live in Saudi Arabia is, "How exotic." They assume that Westerners mingled freely with the Saudis so that it was possible to gain insight into the local way of life.

But Saudis and Westerners were mutually wary: The Saudis afraid of becoming, or even seeming, corrupted by casual association with us; the Westerners afraid of violating some obscure tenet of Shari'a law and getting thrown in jail.

However, the two groups socialized for appearance' sake, each taking pains to be sensitive to the other's customs. ("In Arab culture it is considered rude to sit in such a way as to show the sole of the shoe," advised one company brochure.)

So these get-togethers were dominated by awkward pleasantries, even as they waxed into the night – dinner in Saudi Arabia sometimes not being served until 11 p.m. – since no one was getting drunk. Whenever we went to the house of Nick's boss, his wife (whose limited English worked to the advantage of maintaining distance) invariably said, "You like Jeddah? Jeddah very nice," to which we would nod in agreement. That was it for the rest of the evening.

But even the most banal conversation acquires panache when it's conducted in a palace.

One night Michael invited us to dinner at the house of a Saudi. A few weeks earlier, he'd invited us to another dinner which had been a raucous family affair. So for this gathering, I put on clothes appropriate to a similar occasion, a cotton skirt and blouse.

To get to the L. family compound, we followed Michael's directions which, since most streets didn't have names, relied on landmarks: "Make a right at the Fallopian tubes," (an abstract sculpture,) "another right at the car in the wall." (Sculpture or accident? One couldn't be sure.)

A butler in a long white robe and turban opened the door and led us down the carpeted hallway to a bright, capacious room where two groups sat, the men on the right, the women on the left.

Our hostess, dressed in an expensive silk suit, looked me up and down disparagingly.

"I'm sorry," I said. "I didn't realize this would be such an elegant party."

"That's all right," she said stiffly. "Next time you will be elegant."

Nick and I parted for our respective circles. I sat

with a group of five women who introduced themselves grudgingly before lapsing back into silence.

I addressed one of the less forbidding ones with that classic New York question: "What do you do?"

She shrugged. "And you?"

"I have a son and I'm trying to write a book. How about you?" I looked at the woman next to her.

"I visit my friends. Drink tea."

"Put that in your book," said the third.

An overweight young girl shrugged and said, "I don't do anything. I'm lazy." There was no reason to doubt her.

A college-age girl came down the stairs in a yellow polka dot dress, smiling in an open, friendly way.

"And I study computers," she announced. We talked for a bit before the disapproving silence of the others withered further conversation.

Nick came over and whispered in my ear. "You see that room over there?"

He indicated a small alcove that held a low sofa covered in embroidered pillows. The walls were painted gold.

"That gold is real. The room cost $200,000 to decorate." *[2012 Note: This was in 1987 when gold ranged from $398 to $484 an ounce.]*

As Nick returned to the men's section, the servant came in with a contraption that hissed like an oxygen machine: The hookah, containing a brew made from rotting fruit. I was tempted to try it but noting the communal mouthpiece, declined. Saudi Arabia at that time had an approximately 50% hepatitis A rate.[11]

At midnight, the dining-room opened at last to reveal a groaning board of taboule, mezzah and lamb, all of which was exquisite.

For the second time that evening, our hostess approached, still wearing an expression of disdain. After complimenting her on the spread, I asked about the boutique she ran.

"We have the latest styles from Paris," she said proudly. I wondered what part she'd played in a fashion show in which an Australian friend, Leslie, had modeled since Saudi women weren't allowed to.

"We changed clothes really quickly," Leslie had reported, "so I didn't realize until afterwards that I was wearing a huge purple bow on my bottom."

The butler laid out more plates: hummus with fresh onion and parsley and baba ghanouj.

"Where are your servants from?" I asked Mrs. L., counting four and that was without even setting foot in the kitchen.

"I don't know," she bristled.

"From the Sudan," said her husband. "What about you?"

Ah, someone to talk to!

As Mr. L. and I launched into conversation, an odd object caught my eye: a pastel-colored chandelier shaped like a melting wedding cake.

"My wife did the decorating," Mr. L. explained hastily, wanting to disassociate himself from the eyesore.

We were getting along great which was no doubt why, after ten minutes, he turned on his heels, never to return. Conversation is for form only and must never become animated or gain substance.

The stiff atmosphere even in informal gatherings might have driven foreigners underground for respite but for the godsend of diplomatic immunity. Oases of Western law, Consulates became the Studios 54 of Jeddah, the places everyone clamored to get in since there you could drink with impunity.

Every Thursday night we repaired to one of these, belonging to a country with a reputation for knowing how to have a good time. The annex, furnished with a few wooden counters on which shifty-looking loners perched their beers, had the air of the final outpost of the frontier, its habitues mostly single men in their forties escaping failure back home or, courtesy of a liberal policy towards overseas earnings, working their way out of tax debt. The remaining guests were career expatriot couples, hardy souls who'd been making a home away from home their entire adult lives.

Even here, conversation followed familiar lines: How long have you been in Jeddah? How long are you planning to stay?

But one night after a couple of drinks, Emily told of an unusual encounter: Her radio station had held a competition for Saudi students to write an essay in English. One entrant's family name was Amin. Emily surmised the boy might be the son of former Ugandan President Idi

Amin, known for cannibalism and siccing rats onto the open entrails of his enemies. Once he was ousted from power, Saudi Arabia was the only country that would have him and then, only on condition that he lie low.

"I couldn't resist," Emily said. "I gave the kid a prize. He showed up with his father who was huge; he blocked the doorway. No one recognized him but me. I said, 'Well! Your son certainly speaks wonderful English!'

'You will give him certificate,' he said." Emily imitated his ominous voice.

"'Of course!' I looked in the drawers for any official stamp I could find. *Stamp, stamp, stamp.*"

She replayed the frenzy with which she had gussied up a certificate for the despot's son. The pair left satisfied.

It was at the Consulate that I met Margaret, a British woman married to a salesman. James had been a gifted artist but the Gardners had spent their married life in what Somerset Maugham would have called the "colonies." I once asked James what was the strangest thing he'd ever witnessed during those years. (I, too, was hungry for exotic stories of living abroad.) He thought a moment before answering, "A witch doctor making rain. I suppose he must have had some knowledge of meteorology."

Margaret and I went to the souk (market) a few times together. "I like haggling," she confessed in the back seat of the car as we were driven there by James' company driver.

But as we spent more time together, she said things that rankled. Speaking of riots in the London neighborhood of Brixton she said, "They make their own ghettoes, don't they?"

I was too taken aback to say anything at that moment but after we parted, I mulled over a response.

The opportunity to voice it came soon enough. I asked her about a course she had taken in teaching English as a Second Language.

"Not very good," she said. "But the teacher's name was Hannah Solomon so what do you expect?" She rubbed her thumb and forefinger together.

"I have to ask you to stop making these comments," I said.

"Why?" She didn't bother to feign innocence. "Everyone talks like this, or at least, the honest ones do."

"No they don't although maybe they do in the circles you're used to."

"I'm not talking about you."

"I can't keep going places with you if you talk this way with me."

"I have to be able to speak the way I want. If this affects you personally, tell me and I'll stop. Otherwise, not."

"It does affect me personally."

"How?"

"They're offensive comments. Lots of people in my generation would feel that way." (Margaret was a couple of decades older than I.)

"Look, if this is about you, that's one thing. Otherwise I'll speak the way I like."

We weren't getting anywhere. But a few weeks before, Nick had learned that his boss had been secretly negotiating with another firm; we were going home in three months. I hadn't been allowed to tell anyone but this change in our plans affected my willingness to relax a rule which, up until that moment, had been rigorously observed:

"All right. My father was Jewish."

This was a fact we kept under wraps in Saudi Arabia, since Jews were not allowed in the country. "You could get deported," Nick had said when we first went over and I stoutly said I wasn't going to hide anything. *Deported?* I thought. *Great!* He read my mind: "Or thrown in jail." That had done it. Cowardice prevailed.

"I'm so sorry," Margaret said now, by which she didn't mean, "I'm sorry you're half-Jewish," but, "I'm sorry I said anti-Semitic and other offensive things to you."

In the silence that followed, I could see her replaying our conversations, looking at them in a new light.

"I think you think that everyone's secretly racist except for maybe a few idealists like me," I said.

"I do think that, yes."

She also understood that by letting her in on what needed to be kept secret in Saudi Arabia, I'd placed more trust in her than she'd earned.

"Well, it's very brave of you, being here, isn't it?"

Then, to "repay" me in the currency of confidences, she continued:

"I have a black niece. I don't tell many people that. My brother and his wife adopted her to keep the marriage together."

"Did it work?"

"More or less but it's a terrible reason to have a child; a terrible thing to do to the child."

She spoke with a more vigorous anger than was warranted by any moves her brother and sister-in-law might have made to keep their marriage together.

She took out some pictures of her family including her niece as a little girl.

"Do you make racist remarks in front of your niece?"

"Of course not – it would hurt her. But I'm not a racist. I don't *do* anything to black people or Jews."

The confidences continued.

"I have the feeling I'm waiting for something," she said one day. "You're the only person I've told that to."

"Maybe you're waiting for a grandchild."

"No!"

But I also had the feeling in Saudi Arabia of the suspension of real life.

Another time she reported that the wife of the Y Consul had said, "Jenna looks like Anne Frank." (No one's ever said that before but in Saudi Arabia, any expat who wasn't blond looked like Anne Frank.) "Do you think she might be Jewish?"

"Oh, I shouldn't think so," Margaret had said.

Still, when we went back to the souk together, I refrained from bargaining; didn't want to feed any stereotypical notions she might still be harboring.

One day she gave a lunch at which the subject of

anti-Jewish sentiment in Saudi Arabia came up.

"They're anti-Zionist, not anti-Jewish," said Emily.

"They don't let Jews in the country," I reminded her.

"Oh well, that, yes. But they have a Jewish finance adviser."

She was not being ironic.

For the remainder of our stay in Saudi Arabia, Margaret tried to make up for having behaved like a colonial boor. After a dinner party she said, "I wish you could have been a fly on the wall and heard all the anti-Semitic comments people were making." (*"You see, it is everywhere; it's not just me."*) And when Nick and I went to India, she saw our son every day on the theory that her watchful eye would keep his babysitter in line. He still remembers the M&Ms that she kept in a papier-mâché egg for him.

We took one trip within the Kingdom. As non-Muslims, we weren't allowed in Mecca so we went south to Najran. Since our group of fifteen were the only guests at the hotel, we made friends with the staff who wound up confiding in us how much they got paid: Filipinos earned the most; Sri Lankans, the least. I took Alex to the playground until a band of baboons descended like a rival gang.

The return flight: As we approached Jeddah over the familiar dry, cracked dirt of the desert dotted with scrawny camels, my heart sank in harmony with the descending plane.

Two months later, we were back in New York when I

overheard a conversation on the subway:

"They tried to find a way to keep the raccoons out of the garbage," a young woman said. "But when they came up with a different lock on the lid that stumped the raccoons, it also stumped the tenants."

A far cry from, "Jeddah very nice."

We were home.

Allison

We met at the Women's Center of the compound in Saudi Arabia. A former clothing designer, she now busied herself in needlepoint and interior decorating for which she had the talent of Martha Stewart. She taught me how to dry flowers (hang them upside down in the shade) and how to cut my son's hair (along the length of his head rather than across.)

At fifteen, she had gone to art school. Two years later, she graduated and was hired to decorate the windows of a store on Tokyo's equivalent of 57th Street. Within a year, she was promoted to manager.

A customer asked her to design a line of clothing for his wife. She did. The customer revealed that he had been testing her and invited her to become the top designer at his company in New York.

She was only eighteen and the other employees, jealous that she was their superior, made her job difficult. She married, left the company and had a daughter. Because the couple was still young they went away often, leaving the baby with grandparents. When the child was four, her grandfather who was watching her went inside for "just a minute" and the child ran into the street where she was killed. Allison blamed herself for having so freely left her daughter. The marriage ended.

Three years later Allison married again. She had a boy which relieved her because she was afraid of having another girl. Her third and last child was a girl whom everyone adored.

The Meaning of Chimney

When I was nine and people asked what I wanted to be when I grew up, I said, "Either a baseball player or an archaeologist."

I had another dream which I didn't articulate: To run an orphanage. The details were vague but I think it was in Mexico. Certainly I didn't dream of the actual work involved – repairing the roof or paying the insurance premiums. What I did see were the children who were from all over the world. (This circumstance was also unexplained for surely in a Mexican orphanage, the children would be from only Mexico; I must have been under the influence of a Unicef poster.) I would turn up in the playground – for some reason, in the fantasy I am a monk in a brown robe – and the children would run to me in excitement.

When my son was in third grade, he entered a parochial school in Brooklyn. The school sent a questionnaire asking if parents had any special skills we'd like to pass on to the children. I offered to teach English as a second language. I had a theory that a child from a foreign country needed only a slight push to make friends at which point his or her English would take off.

I started with three third graders: Irma, from Jordan: Rita from Sri Lanka and Jessica from the Philippines.

Irma reminded me of my old school motto, Bravely and Correctly. She was frequently incorrect but all the braver for it. She dominated the group; I didn't have to coax conversation out of her. But her reading was surprisingly hesitant. The confident pre-teen who, accustomed to caring for younger siblings, was frequently paper and pencil provider to the group, became a trembling child. Rita spoke less but read better. Jessica understood well, read the best of the three and didn't say a word. Sometimes after Irma had been telling us a long story – her family provided material worthy of the Arabian Nights – I looked around to see if Jessica was paying attention and found that she wasn't there at all. Usually she was under the table, hiding.

Irma had trouble spelling. Arabic is one of those languages that are written like shorthand, omitting short vowels. Irma found it hard to break the habit so "hurdle" became "hrdl," "garbage," because of her pronunciation, "garbtch." All the children spelled words as they pronounced them which is a good idea in principle although in their case it could be a problem. Jessica pronounced "p" and "f" interchangeably. I had heard that the Philippines has many dialects of which two are Filipino and Pilipino. That sounds like the beginning of a joke for which Jessica could one day write the punch line, for alarming things happened when she read words like "hockey puck" or "phoenix." (Apparently, Pilipino was an experiment by Ferdinand Marcos to rid the national language of foreign influence.[12]) Irma pronounced, "I eat it," "I it it" and spelled accordingly. I tried to get the children to come up with words that rhymed with "eat." They were silent.

"What are these?" I asked, pointing to Irma's feet.
"Shoes."

"And what's inside the shoes?"

"Socks."

"And what's inside the socks?"

"Rubber bands."

"Feet!" I cried.

"Oh, yes," marveled Rita.

"Fit!" exclaimed Irma.

Rita didn't care about spelling or any other schoolwork. She took pains over her handwriting but when she finished an assignment, she walked around looking for trouble and sabotaging the progress of the others.

One day she worked on a book report which began, "My name Rita West. This stores about a girl name Margret."

"Why did you tell us your name?" I asked. "You already wrote it up here." I pointed at the top right-hand corner of the page.

"She introduce herself," Irma explained. "I tol' her that's not what 'Introduction' mean but she doesn't listen."

Through the distorting lens of their language difficulties, the children perceived a bizarre world. When we read a Berenstain Bears story, Rita asked, "What does that mean – 'Mamma Bear raised her eyebrows,' – she pulls them?" And she pulled her own.

"She count them?" said Irma.

The children loved to play games but when that got boring, we talked.

It wasn't always easy to come up with a topic of conversation, especially once Irma's family saga ended.

Rita described her nightmares of devils tempting her to watch television instead of doing her homework.

While they hadn't made any more friends in the classroom, the children were at least getting to know each other and have more fun in school.

Classes in grade school often fall into the patterns of feudalism. At the apex of the pyramid is the class brain who functions as King or Queen. Beneath him or her are several noblemen who dominate various provinces: One may play the violin; another, tennis. One does science projects involving working batteries; several may already know Spanish; one is the class clown. Beneath these are all the rest who may in time reveal their own more esoteric provinces. At the bottom is the criminal who is always in trouble.

My students were outside the pyramid entirely. They were in the classroom what they were in the world: foreigners and as such, treated with benign neglect. Rita, because she rarely knew what was going on, sometimes deviated into the role of criminal. Someone accused her of having "cooties," and the stigma stuck.

When I was in fourth grade, an English girl joined our class. She was clever, pretty and a teacher's pet so we hated her. I was a leader in the campaign to make her life miserable. The following year, my family moved to England and the tables turned. Someone wrote on the schoolyard wall, "Yankee Go Home." I learned to say, "Crikey" and, "Cor Blimey" and keep a stiff upper lip. By the time we moved back to New York four years later, I was like a bird contaminated by human scent – I no longer fit in here, either. Even now in any given society, I identify mostly with the outsider.

I wanted to step in to defend Rita in the classroom. But when she dressed up for class outings and the other kids, all in jeans, stared at her, she only shrugged. She had more integrity at nine than I could have dreamed of. Likewise Irma who on one class trip wore a dress that was so frilly, someone asked if she was in fact wearing two dresses. Irma didn't even shrug: Thrilled with her dress, she sashayed dreamily, oblivious to the snickers of her classmates. Or perhaps she wasn't oblivious; she simply dismissed their comments as jealousy and perhaps she was right. I began to understand why my students were slower than I had expected to pick up English; at some level, they had made the wiser choice.

Still, it was good news when Jessica reported that she had made two friends outside our group. But she didn't talk to them; she only listened. I gave her the assignment of talking to her friends. A week later, she said that she had. I believed her because now she talked to me.

Christmas provided new fuel for our conversations. Rita had never seen snow, "except in the refrigerator." She was afraid of Santa Claus because she thought he might take her in exchange for the toys. Irma didn't know much about Christmas because she didn't celebrate it; Jessica eagerly filled her in. Rita interrupted to protest as though on one of the finer points of philosophy:

"But," she gestured with long, be-ringed fingers, "I

do not understand the meaning of 'chimney.'"

Irma's spelling evolved one syllable at a time. "Hrdl" was now "herdl." I explained about the "e" at the end and forgot about the one Irma had put at the beginning. My identification with my students was now complete: Having stepped through the looking-glass, I'd forgotten how to spell.

In March, a topic of conversation landed on us like a grenade: Rita's parents were planning to send her back to Sri Lanka to boarding school with her older brother. Her parents would remain here. For holidays she would go to her grandparents. Why had Rita's parents hatched this plan?

"So we don't get spoiled."

That's for sure. Alone on the other side of the world sure doesn't sound like being smothered.

"What do you mean, 'spoiled?'"

"So we don't take drugs and run away." I began to sympathize with Rita's parents but still...

Her parents were unhappy with her grades. In fact, Rita's teacher had struggled to show her in the best light. When her work fell below an acceptable level, she received NG for No Grade rather than F.

Rita didn't want to leave her parents. She had seen the boarding school and didn't like it.

"The food have worms," she said. I thought of Oliver Twist, my orphan fantasy suddenly all too real.

During the next set of parent-teacher conferences, Rita's teacher discussed the boarding school plan with her parents and told them Rita was doing much better. The teacher had devised new tests for her so she could give her a real grade. In an effort to appease Rita's parents, I also submitted grades for my students. Rita got a proud B.

Irma was now a profusion of vowels. In fact, "fusion" was one of the words on her spelling list; she spelled it "fiyoujun." "Logical" was "lajgickle." I detected progress. Rita spelled "logical" "largecoal" and I wondered what she thought it meant. Jessica now talked all the time. She was so fluent I wondered if her spoken English, like Jessica herself, had only been hiding. On a history test she got a hundred.

At the end of the year, Rita's parents decided not to send their children to Sri Lanka alone. Instead the whole family moved out of the city.

The following year, as though someone had shaken a kaleidoscope, I had a different configuration of students. When my son needed a pitcher, I understood the purpose of my baseball career when I was nine. As for archaeology, the past I dug up was my own.

Call of the Wild? Wrong Number

Last May, my husband bought a tent. [This article was written before our divorce and, believe it or not, had nothing to do with it.] Soon after, oddly-shaped packages started arriving in the mail: sleeping bags, a kerosene lamp, the parts for a stove. I didn't like the thought they conjured up: Nick was planning to take us camping. I said nothing. Then one evening he came home waving something in his hand as though he'd been dealt three aces. What he was actually holding were three tickets to Vancouver, dated the last day of school.

I'd never been camping. Camping scared me. I like animals but not in my bed. It wasn't raccoons or chipmunks that were the problem; no one's ever been eaten by a chipmunk. It was bears. After bears came wolves, ticks, snakes... It wasn't just animals, either. There was getting lost, driving off a mountain road... Then there was Miscellaneous – dangers I didn't know of yet but *that* wouldn't stop them from happening.

I've lived in New York most of my life. I'm pale, aspired in high school to be an intellectual and have been called neurotic by people who wanted me to do something I didn't want to do. They understate the case: I'm not neurotic; I'm a coward. I feel the world to be a minefield of hidden dangers waiting to snap up the unsuspecting. Fear, then, is an ally. In fact, fear is the great underrated emotion. It keeps rabbits away from predators and watchful humans away from dangerous situations like camping.

Thus I get no thrill from a risk conquered; I prefer a risk avoided. But our son Alex was excited about the trip and least of all did I want him to go without me.

"Oh, come on," Nick said. "Everybody goes camping. What do you want to do – keep Alex in the hot, filthy city all summer? It's beautiful out there. There are all kinds of animals; nobody ever sees a bear. People go camping for years who *want* to see bears – the bears run away."

This may have been true but it was also irrelevant. Sure, there were families who loved camping and returned without scars from bear attacks. But Nick wouldn't want to do it the way they did. From the glint in his eye, the way he'd planned the trip for months without mentioning it, calling for catalogues and investing in gear for the serious camper – a device to sanitize mountain water, an assortment of knives each of which I imagined in his hand, stabbing a bear through the heart – it was alarmingly clear that a tame family outing was not all he had in mind.

At the company Christmas party, one of Nick's colleagues had described his vacation in Alaska. It was beautiful, he had said.

"Yeah, but I wouldn't do what he did, all that tourist crap, camp sites, all that," Nick had said afterwards. "I'd go where there's nobody, just Nature."

The colleague had told us that it was possible to register with the Rangers and trek deep into the wilds on your own. If you didn't return within three days of the date you'd put down in the Visitors' book, they went looking for you.

"There's rafting, kayaks," Nick went on, dreamily.

Oh, God, I thought, *Alex can't even swim.*

"Alex could see the animals..." Nick had a faraway smile as he said this, with a hint of mischief at the corner.

And suppose the animals want a closer relationship than just being seen? I thought.

The more enthusiastic Nick became, the more I balked inside. An occasional perusal of the obituary pages informs the reader that the death rate from accidents seems to go up during summer vacations: Drownings, climbing accidents... When people go to unfamiliar places and act as carefree as when they're home, dire things can happen. But I didn't say anything; an argument would only have tightened Nick's position.

For a month after that, Nick had talked of Alaska. He brought home Jack London stories for Alex who was then eight. I hoped something would turn up to distract him from his new project.

Nick doesn't take life lightly. He works hard and wants the other parts of his life to make his work worthwhile. He wants to have something to show for his time on earth: to see, do, all he can of what the world has to offer. To this end, he boldly goes where few men have gone before, at least, if they can help it: He volunteered for the Air Force during the Vietnam War.

It was the highlight of his life. He was shot; he shot others, earning medals which we find at the back of the closet whenever we move and which he gazes at lovingly before closing them again in their black cases. For years, whenever we made a new acquaintance, Nick found a way to mention his flying days in the X Division in Vietnam.

Even now, every so often he exercises those death-defying muscles, driving at twenty miles over the speed limit, or dashing across fifty-seventh street in the middle of the block in the middle of the day. At these times, I don't like myself or Alex to be with him.

Nothing did turn up to distract Nick from his latest obsession, his newest raison d'etre; not even money – he had frequent flier miles. We were going to Alaska.

I threw a fit. I'd given in on where we lived, how our apartment was decorated, what we did on weekends, what we watched on T.V. With Alaska, I cashed in my chips – I sobbed.

"All right," Nick said. "I'll find something more family oriented; a little closer to home, maybe Vancouver, O.K?"

I nodded. The "closer to home" line was a joke – it isn't direct flights that save you from bears – but "family-oriented" meant he would consider staying at a campsite.

"OK."

For a month, nothing more was said. Nick flew to Tokyo on a trip that was too speculative to be considered business and I wondered if he'd used his frequent flier miles for it which would turn the camping-out-west idea back into a dream.

Then May arrived and with it, the unfamiliar

packages and the tickets.

I decided to learn about camping. Not to get into the spirit of the thing but in the belief that this was the only way we would survive. Nick brought home books to see what there was to do in the Vancouver area. I went straight to the index and looked up "bears."

The books advised as follows:

If you meet a black bear walk backwards, waving your arms to show him you're not a deer. Speak in low tones. If he "displays signs of aggression" you should "look big" but not look him in the eye. Hit him on the snout with a long stick. If you meet a grizzly, do the opposite: Play dead and cover your neck with your hands.

I interpreted this last instruction to mean that grizzlies were more aggressive than black bears and would probably attack; so protect your spine and hope you get off without paralysis.

The crucial question, it seemed then, was how to tell a black bear from a grizzly. Black bears are not always black. They can be brown or blond. I called the Rangers' station in Vancouver.

Black bears' snouts are shorter than grizzlies', the ranger said. Black bears do not have the skulking gait of grizzlies that comes from the protruding bone in the grizzlies' necks.

This was useful information if the bear was on all fours when you met him and didn't have his back to you. And that's assuming I could tell a long snout from a short one.

I asked the ranger how to keep bears away, especially while you're asleep.

"Keep a campfire going."

"How do you do that?"

But he wouldn't answer. He had his own agenda of fears and forest fires ranked near the top. *Forest fires* popped onto my mental list of risks.

"Nine times out of ten," the ranger continued before signing off, "they're more afraid of you than you are of them."

Perhaps as a concession, Nick also bought a book called First Aid in the Wilderness. There were headings for Frostbite, Rabies and Giardiasis, a word that had only recently entered my vocabulary but was becoming uncomfortably familiar. I learned to be suspicious of sparkling streams. Giving form to my fear of Miscellaneous, there were also references to mountain lions and coyotes. In a final flourish of realizing the reader's worst nightmare, the authors provided instructions on how to amputate your own leg. They sounded casual about it as though, if you were reading the section with more than passing interest, the leg was probably frozen so you didn't have to worry about the absence of anesthesia.

All the books said that if you saw "traces of bear," — a clawed tree or bear skat, for instance – you should leave the area.

The last day of school arrived, a Friday; we flew to Vancouver. We had been there before and I hadn't been impressed. But now as we rented a car and left the city for the wilderness, I looked back with longing. Its provincial sterility receded like a loved one I'd never see again.

For the next few days, I was unusually indulgent of whims. If the others wanted to make a side-trip – to any museum however dusty, any go-cart park however rusty, – I exclaimed, "Ooh yeah! Maybe they have a steam engine!" and, "Anyone want to race?" Alex couldn't believe I let him play all the pinball games he wanted. But each night that Nick got tired of driving and swung into the parking lot of a motel was one less night outdoors. Eventually, however, we were in the mountains.

Along the way to the campsite Nick had circled on the map as our destination, we stopped at restaurants and gas stations. At each, I debriefed people about bears. How many were there? Where? What time of day?

Some people mistook this curiosity for a desire to see a bear. For I was like Captain Ahab in pursuit of his respective animal. When I told them No, just the opposite, they said, "Don't worry. Nine times out of ten they're more afraid of you than you are of them." This implied that the frightened bear would behave as a frightened human being might and run away. But what I knew about animals said that that was not how they always behaved when frightened.

Everyone had a bear story. One couple had stopped to help a baby bear that had been hit by a car. They were attacked by the mother. A ranger had seen two tourists who had covered their child's face with honey to attract a bear for pictures. They were at too low an altitude for bears;

the experiment failed. (This ranger also said he'd known tourists to pick up a handful of snow with the idea of taking it home as a souvenir.) The cook in one of the restaurants we ate in had been attacked when he walked home in his work clothes.

And everyone had advice:

"Throw something to distract the bear." "Don't throw anything; you might annoy it. Climb a tree." "Don't climb a tree; bears can climb trees."

A waiter told us of his uncle who had climbed a tree, pursued by a bear. The bear climbed after him. The man leapt to the branch of a neighboring tree. The bear, sizing up the situation and seeing that he would break the branch if he followed the man, climbed down the first tree and up the second. The man leapt back to the first tree. Man and bear went back and forth until someone else came along and the bear gave up.

The tree-climbing advice became academic since in the two weeks we were in Canada, I didn't see a tree any of us could climb. They were all flagpoles without branches for at least twenty feet. And the branches they did have were the frail ones of Christmas trees.

"Wear bearbells." "Bear bells are too gentle; carry a radio." "Whistle." "Don't whistle; you'll sound like a marmot, which bears hunt. Shout." "Don't shout; you'll sound angry." "Don't wear perfume." "Don't wear fruity perfume." (Nobody explained what that was.) *"Don't carry fruit or use perfumed soap." "Don't use lip balm." "Don't carry meat, salmon or tuna fish sandwiches."*

"Don't get your period." *"Walk downwind so the bears can smell you and you don't surprise them."* *"Walk upwind so the bears can't smell you."*

"How do you know which way the wind is blowing?" I asked a ranger who was of the downwind persuasion.

"Look at the trees."

"They don't move."

"Generally the wind goes with the sun; up the mountain as the sun rises; down as it sets."

This was more useful but it, too, was academic since if you were downwind when you started your walk, you'd be upwind coming back.

"Don't have a dog." *"Cook fifty yards from your camp and change your clothes before you go to bed."*

One thing people did agree on was bear spray, a mace-like substance, so we went shopping for some.

I'd never been in an outdoorsman's store but since it was another reprieve from camping, I savored every fleeting moment. For fishermen, there was leech yarn and shiny thread with tell-it-like-it-is names such as Worm Green and Cow Dung Olive; Bucktail from Umpqua Feather Merchants and a book called The Art of Tying the Nymph. We bought two cans of bear spray and a bear bell each to wear around our necks like lepers and warn the bears away.

Outside, two women were talking as they headed for their car:

"Grandpa died. Then Grandma died. She wanted to

be cremated. Afterwards, they found Grandpa in the trunk of the car. She didn't want to go anywhere without him, I guess. Five or six years later. He'd been there the whole time."

I could almost get into this camping business if it wasn't for the shadow of death hanging over us.

"Anybody hungry?" Nick said, revving up the car. "There should be someplace nearby we can stop and cook some lunch."

"All right," I said, "but you have to change your clothes before we go to bed, then."

"Why?"

"The bears can smell what you've been cooking."

"Aw, come on, where'd you pick that one up?"

I got out the book and presented Nick the relevant passage. By way of response, he swerved onto the driveway of a nearby Great Western.

A busload of Japanese tourists had just arrived and, on their way to the restaurant, stopped to watch something in the grass. Alex ran ahead to see what was going on.

A tribe of ground squirrels were diving over each other into an underground highway of tunnels. More and more squirrels appeared, like hidden pictures in a drawing for children. Alex was mesmerized.

Inside the restaurant, while Nick and I read the menu, Alex looked intently out the window.

"Twenty-three, twenty-four, twenty-five..." he murmured to himself.

"What are you counting?" I asked. "Ground

squirrels?"

"No," he said. "Japanese tourists."

The meal over, he wiped his hands on his pants.

"What – !" I cried. "Don't do that!"

He looked up in alarm; I don't usually make a fuss about messiness.

"You have to change those before you sleep outdoors."

"O.K., Mamma," he quavered, more scared of me than of the creature that was causing my alarm.

Walking back to the car, I lingered over the ground squirrels, exclaiming, "Ooh, look at that one! Isn't this great?" With what now seems like touching optimism, I hoped to distract the others, thereby putting off – maybe even preventing – our encounter with larger game. But Nick was not to be sidetracked.

"Come on," he said, without breaking stride towards the parking lot whose inviting, manmade concrete I gazed at with the fondness of a departing lover.

We drove another three hours, or rather, Nick drove. A corollary of my born and bred New Yorkerhood is that I can't drive. I sometimes feel guilty about that on vacations. But not on this one, with Nick leading us up the mountain of Death.

Through the window, Canada really did look like its pictures in National Geographic, vastly green and boring. *Maybe we'll reach the campsite too late to pitch our tent – that'll give us one more night at a motel!*

Shortly before dusk we arrived at the site Nick had

been heading for.

The camp was Edenesque. As Nick got the tent out of the car, I looked around, determined not to pitch in and make it any easier for him to put our lives at risk.

Stellar jays hopped on the lowest branch of the pine under which we were to sleep. A chipmunk stared before darting into a hole; a long-eared rabbit crossed from stage left. A scene out of Disney. You could almost hear the Pastorale Symphony swelling with the smell of pine. In the middle of the campsite stood a tall tree fragment like a hooded St. Francis preaching to the surrounding fauna. The beauty of the place banished all fear: Nothing bad could happen here. That night, on one of our newly acquired inflatable mattresses, with a sense of surrendering to Fate under the canopy of outer space, I slept well.

The following morning, wearing our bear bells and carrying our canisters of bear spray, we drove to a nearby trail for a hike where every ten feet I shouted in bold but cheerful tones a paraphrase of the Act Up chant: "We're here; we're not deer. Get used to it."[1]

There was no wild life in the woods visible to the naked eye: Not a squirrel; not even a pigeon. Then, as we rounded the path back to the road, we came upon a pile of bear skat.

"Let's hurry up," I pleaded, remembering the advice of the guide books. Since we were heading out anyway, no one complained.

---

1   The Act Up chant went: "We're here; we're queer; get used to it."

On the way back to camp, we were stopped by the Royal Canadian Mounted Police. They were mounted in a white police car.

"What's that?" asked the officer, pointing at the bear spray that lay next to Nick on the front seat. "Give it to me nice and slow."

Nick did as he was told. He's been stopped for speeding in twenty-six states and knows how to treat cops.

Weighing the can, the cop said, "Do you know what this is? This is a concealed weapon. What are you doing with this?"

"We're camping," I said, eager to oblige him. "It's to use if a bear comes. You'll give it back to us, won't you?"

"Why, ma'am? Ninety-nine times out of a hundred they're more afraid of you than you are of them."

He was the sixth person to tell me that but none of them knew how afraid I was. And anyway, afraid or not, the bear was stronger than I was. I refrained from pointing this out to the cop.

"Do you have any other weapons in the car?"

Nick shook his head. I thought of the knives, the hatchet and the other can of bear spray.

"Any other bear spray?"

"Yes, I have some bear spray," I offered.

"Where is it?"

"In here." I patted my pocket.

"Could you give me that please?"

I, too, am interested in staying on the right side of the police. With an impulsive flourish as though of generosity,

205

I handed over our sole immediate defense against bear attack.

The cop read the label, lectured us some more, wrote out a ticket and returned the small can of bear spray though not the big one.

It was dusk. There was no place within a hundred miles where we could replace the bear spray.

Tuesday: another drive; another hike, this time to Bear Creek.

As it turned out, this was no whimsical name. Immediately, we encountered bear skat.

"Let's go," I pleaded again.

Not only do the guide books advise you to leave the area when you see bear skat. (*Ah! But in which direction should you go?*) They also tell you to avoid running water where you cannot easily hear bears approaching.

"Just give it another five minutes," said Nick.

Thirty feet away was another pile of bear skat – and another and another. Either a bear lived nearby or a mother had recently passed through with her cubs. Hard to know which option was more distasteful.

As we drove back to camp, Nick planned the afternoon's hike.

"OK," he said upon winding up that happy task, "where do you want to go for lunch?"

(*"OK,"* I heard. *"We've set the date of execution. What'll we have for our last meal?"*)

"It doesn't matter," I said.

The afternoon brought reprieve. The car putt-putted

and we had to drive to town to get it fixed.

That night I was haunted by the perennial question that overcomes timid campers in the woods: *To pee or not to pee.* I decided not.

The next morning, we woke up at six in order to be on time for a horseback expedition Nick had arranged while in town.

"I'm going to the bathroom," Alex said, and he headed towards the wooden hut.

I'm overprotective, I thought, *but what the hell? I'll go with him.*

In the foliage, a large black shape stumbled around.

"Ah yes, a homeless person rummaging for cans," I thought, ever the New Yorker in a state of denial.

The shape stood up.

The postcard I wrote to my mother later that day read:

Alex and I were on our way to the bathroom this morning when what did we see twenty feet away but a BIG BEAR.

He was over six feet as he leaned with both paws against the trunk of the tree. In his ear was a red tag. He looked at us with curiosity like someone at a party who's open to conversation.

"Mommy," I whimpered. As somebody remarked later, it showed where my faith lay.

For reasons I have mulled over ever since, I decided

the best place to be was in the bathroom with a solid door between us and the bear. To get there, however, we had to pass him. Alex was trudging ahead, oblivious of the creature he was about to walk by. Did he think the bear was supposed to be there? (which wouldn't have been such an unreasonable thought.) I didn't want to call out to him.

What I did next is a road map of what you're not supposed to do: I grabbed Alex's hand and ran past the bear to the men's room which lay straight ahead, closer than the ladies'. When we were at the door, I remembered the advice from one of the outdoors books, turned around waving my arms and pleaded, "We're humans."

The bear stared with the uncomprehending yellow eyes of a drunk. There was no getting through to him. Dumb animal. We ran inside and I cranked open the window.

"Get the bear spray," I shouted to Nick, waking the rest of the camp. The sounds of a tin orchestra started up as campers banged pots and pans to scare the bear away. If he was more afraid of us than we were of him, he put on a good show of nonchalance. He sniffed a tent in which a half-naked couple clutched each other, Nick said later, for with spray in hand, he'd gone in pursuit of a confrontation.

"I apologized," Nick said, "but they were French-Canadian. They said, 'Ees all right, – Please do not go.'"

Nick didn't get the chance to use the bear spray. A lanky, stooped man who looked like a woodsman in a fairy-tale fired a blank shot. The bear took the hint and ambled off.

"He probably came during the night and fell asleep there," said the ranger when we reported the incident at breakfast. "They're nocturnal animals."

Score one for the decision to forego that middle-of-the-night trip to the bathroom.

"Was it a black bear?"

"Yes."

"Huh! You're lucky. They're usually more aggressive."

Another piece of information I was glad not to have had at the time.

"You say he had a red tag?"

"Yes."

"Yeah; they do that when the bear's causing problems. It's like when you're a kid in school, you get a bad mark; the next time, you get detention? If a bear's acting like that, we gotta shoot 'im. Well, thanks for stopping in. We'll send somebody after 'im."

I got no satisfaction from this. My quarrel with bears was nothing personal.

Over breakfast, Nick studied the map, turning every so often to his sidekick, the guidebook.

"We're not too far from the coast. What do you say we pack up, then after riding, go down, maybe see some whales."

Coast?! Civilization!

"O.K."

Bears live at high altitudes. Heading for sea level, surely we would be leaving them behind, forever. I realized now that in spite of the line Nick had taken back in New York, – "There are all kinds of animals out there; nobody ever sees a bear; people go camping for years who *want* to see bears; the bears run away," – the rabbits and the ground squirrels had been, for him, irrelevant. Seeing a bear had been Nick's purpose in the trip itself as well as in all the hikes. It was Nick who was Captain Ahab. Now that we had seen our bear, he wanted to move on. He'd get no argument from this corner.

But in every sense of the expression, we weren't out of the woods yet. First, there was the morning's agenda.

Nick had described it as a ride "up the mountain," offering spectacular views. That probably meant standing at the edge of a cliff but I was willing to check it out.

We arrived at the ranch, Beaver Hill, at nine. Two brothers in their early twenties saddled the horses for The Ride of the City Slickers.

"What's the trail like?" I asked Clay, the older brother, who was going to lead the ride of about ten visitors.

"We go up the mountain, come back, take about three hours."

"Is there anything on it that might be dangerous for a nine-year-old?"

"Nah."

"How wide is the mountain path?"

"What do you mean?"

"Five feet? Ten?"

"Ten."

"What about if the horse slips?"

"Horses don't slip." He smiled at the absurd thought and we mounted the snorting mares.

"Don't worry," said the ranch-hand who was weather-beaten, smoking and had what doctors call a "productive" cough. "These horses won't do nothin' wrong."

Clay's horse reared.

"The only problem is that one," the ranch-hand amended, cocking his head in Clay's direction, "but Clay'll take care of him."

However, Clay's horse had other ideas. In a move that was reminiscent of a slingshot, he backed up before setting off in a gallop across the meadow.

"Whoa!" shouted Clay, kicking the horse which ignored him. Clay slapped and yanked the reins until the horse settled down to a trot, muttering. But now my horse darted across the field after Clay's as I flopped in the saddle, pulling the reins. The horse tossed his head but returned to the fold. However, I took the incident as an omen.

"Ready?" said Clay.

"No, the boy and I will go on a separate trail."

This time nobody protested. Alex and I dismounted and watched the caravan sidle off through the trees without us.

After Dell, the younger brother, finished breakfast and gave a good-bye kiss to a high school girl whom, up until that moment, I'd taken to be his sister, Alex and I followed him to the stable to find suitable horses for our tour of the forest. No mountains. The ranch-hand gave us each a retired nag and Dell's horse was without eccentricity.

The forest was dappled with patches of light thrown onto white birch trunks. A mother and baby grouse fluttered up, startled at our approach.

Alex's horse had an equine version of a compulsive eating disorder and stopped every few feet to munch. As her head was buried in her fourth bush, Alex whispered, "Look!"

Thirty feet away stood a deer, watching us like a child who is unaccustomed to strangers. Her curiosity satisfied, she turned and trotted off into the thicket with her tail up.

"She mooned us," said Alex in delight, as we resumed our ride.

"Does your family own this part of the woods?" I asked Dell, after a pause.

"Yep."

"Do you ever get bored being here year 'round?"

"Nope."

The phrase "laconic cowboy" came to mind.

"Do you see lots of bear around here?"

"Nope. One came 'round a few weeks ago. Haven't seen any since then."

I told him our bear story but he wasn't impressed. I remembered the girl he had kissed good-bye and figuring that was where his mind was going to stay, gave up on conversation.

We got back to the ranch at noon, a few minutes before Nick and company.

"You would have killed them," Nick giggled as we left the stable for the main house. "The path up the mountain was about three feet wide and it was fifteen hundred feet down."

Grim relief settled in, swiftly followed by "*What if…*" scenarios: *What if my horse had shied while we were in the woods? Would we have stayed there alone until the others came back? What if the horse waited until we were halfway up the mountain?*

After lunch we got back in the car where, as we wound our way down the mountain, the prospect of returning to sea level beckoned, like disembarking from a plane.

Through the window, the clouds moved evenly in fixed relation to each other as though on a glass pane except for one which, impaled on a distant peak, got left behind.

Half way down the mountain, Nick spotted a makeshift airport. Two-seaters and airplanes that looked as though they were made of balsa wood and Elmer's glue sat in the grass like large hornets. A homemade sign advertised, "Soaring."

The Vietnam gleam dancing in his eye, Nick swung the car onto the driveway, got out and conferred with a man in the hangar who apparently ran the place. He returned to the car with a grin:

"They only have one rate – seventy-five dollars for all three of us."

"You can go."

"It's the same if we all go."

"Uh-uh."

"Just me and Alex?"

"Uh-uh."

"It only takes half an hour."

Time was not the issue. As far as I was concerned, we had all too much time on this vacation. Height was the issue.

"You can go."

Nick returned to the man and took out his wallet, beckoning to us to get out of the car.

"'Be back in half an hour," he called over his shoulder as he went off with the man, talking of flying exploits.

Sitting at a picnic table, Alex and I watched the two get into the plane which headed over the mountain. Alex grabbed my hand though not in fear – it was the linked-finger grasp that signaled the onset of a thumb-wrestling match.

What is it about airports that makes them so windy – the wide open space? I mused as Alex, lifting his elbow off the table, won eleven of our first thirteen games. *Echoes of bygone flights?*

A plane landed and the pilot emerged, passing our table on his way to the office. Nodding towards his plane I asked, "Would you mind telling me what this does to your insurance premiums?"

"Who cares?" he tossed back over his shoulder as he

swaggered off.

More thumb-wrestling. The pilot came out of the office, returning to our table.

"It's really very safe," he confided. "It's just when you get into winds you can find yourself in trouble."

"Is this windy?"

"Not here. But up in the mountains the winds are three times what they are here. Then it gets like water rushing over rocks. It forms eddies."

Nick's plane returned and Nick got out, feverish with excitement.

"You should have come," he gushed. "It was beautiful. There's no engine, it's completely quiet."

I've heard quiet, I thought.

"You've got to live."

"Yes, that is what I would like to do."

We ate dinner that night at a pizza parlor where the waitress had the wide, wrinkled face and straight black hair of a Native Canadian. A look around confirmed that the other employees were Native, too.... And the clientele: Groups of teenagers, families, a homeless man: all Native.

On the notice board were the business card of a Dr. Freesailing, Dentist, and a bulletin that read:

Nuu Chah Nulth Tribal Council. Ohiaht, Hesquiat, Toquaht. The Miss Nuu-Chah-Nulth Princess Pageant.

Look forward to letting Toastmaster build your self-confidence.

Self-defense, elders.

*May be required: Attend Fall Fair Treaty
Negotiations Meetings. First Nation Festival.*

Signed,

*April Titian
Kleco-Kleco.*

If countrysides could be described as prosperous, Canada's would be at the top of the charts. The Native Canadians seemed incongruously poor.

We had seen no minorities since leaving New York, no immigrants of any background either among the Canadians or even the tourists. The Native Canadians seemed to have taken on the role of local minority, as though somebody's got to do it.

It had been a relaxed day ending in the ultimate indulgence: sleeping indoors at the Fairfield Inn.

Next morning, the General Store-cum-diner downstairs bristled with the hiss of salmon cakes.

"Where' you from?" asked the teenage waiter as he set down pancakes for Nick and Alex and a muffin for me.

"New York."

"Really? What part?"

"Brooklyn."

"Brooklyn!? Really?"

"Mm hmm."

"Is it like the movies?"

What did he mean? A Tree Grows in Brooklyn?

Spike Lee?

"What do you mean?"

"You know, like... Well, it's sort of scummy, isn't it?" he gushed in a spurt of chutzpah to overcome his embarrassment. "Wow! I never thought I'd meet anyone from Brooklyn. Did you ever go to Lower Manhattan and see the David Letterman show on the Sony screen?" He probably meant Times Square. "Do you know who David Letterman is?"

I debated telling him I knew two people who worked on Letterman but decided that although it might make his day, it was cheap.

"Yes."

"Is Canada what you expected? Everyone thinks it's really cold. It's not. It's just that American weather is Fahrenheit and Canadian is Celsius."

While Alex finished breakfast, Nick went outside. My antennae sprang into alert-mode: *What's he arranging now?*

A rack of leaflets on the counter detailed the activities in the area; the most eye-catching one featuring a picture of excited people in red rubber suits standing like a row of shiny devils aboard a medium-sized motorboat, their hair blown back. This represented the area's foremost tourist attraction: Whale-watching; the red suits a precaution in case the whale-watcher fell over the low railing into the ocean. Or maybe a whale could overturn the boat; we were still in Nature-country, a long way from home.

Time for the first of the day's thumb-wrestling tournaments: Sixty-three to four, favor Alex, by the time Nick returned.

"Come on," he said. "We're going whale-watching. The boat leaves in ten minutes. Get in the car."

The trip was triumphant: The boat (which was of imposing dimensions) came within fifty feet of a family of whales, in violation of Canadian law but thrilling the tourists. I crouched on deck, choosing cold over the nausea that ballooned when I went inside.

"Where' you from?" said the captain.

"Brooklyn."

"What's your name?"

The answer was overtaken by a retch.

"So, Brooklyn," the captain said, kindly, when we had docked, "I hope it was worth it."

"Oh yes," I answered with the fervor of gratitude to be back on solid ground.

Next on the agenda was a fishing expedition. We would find someone with a motor-boat to take us out to catch salmon or whatever else the local waters offered.

"Just make sure they have a life-vest Alex' size," I said.

"O.K."

While Nick arranged for a boat, I slipped into the fishing tackle shop next door. Time was short so I got to the point.

"Have there ever been cases of a whale overturning a boat?"

"No, they're very gentle," assured the man behind the counter. "One motorboat even cut a whale but it didn't come after the boat. Really, they're more afraid of you than you are of them."

I knew whales were gentle, (except transients who eat sea-lions and other mammals and who, presumably, wouldn't turn up their noses at a human.) But at a cocktail party at the Vancouver Aquarium on our previous trip, a marine biologist had said that with the gentlest of intentions, a whale might bounce a human on the ocean floor in play.

"Are there sharks?"

The man shrugged.

"Haven't heard of any."

This wasn't reassuring. I stood there like Mike Wallace, waiting for the uncomfortably long silence to elicit an admission. A customer with a German accent obliged what seemed to be my need for sharks.

"There are basking sharks," he offered tentatively, as though they might not count. The name conjured up sharks that lay around sunbathing on the rocks instead of hunting.

Sharks – Check.

Nick returned, breathless with excitement.

"O.K., it's all set. I got us a fourteen-foot motor boat and it has a small vest for Alex."

We headed out to the dock where the owner of the boat was rummaging in the cupboard.

"Everybody's here," Nick said to his large behind.

The fisherman emerged with a battered life vest.

His face was grizzled with grey and, I noted with sinking optimism, his stomach of Santa Claus-like dimensions.

"Haven't used this, five, six years," he said, dusting the vest off and handing it to Alex. It was indeed Small but for a small adult. We put it on Alex anyway.

"Bill," said the fisherman, holding out his hand. "Sit over there." He indicated the back of the boat. "Later you can help me drive," he added to Alex.

"Are you certified in life-saving?" I asked, casual as ever.

"What?"

I repeated the question.

He laughed and pulled the cord, revving up the motor.

"I am," said Nick and we vroomed out to sea.

Crystal spray leapt into the air as the boat shattered the water, Alex leaning over the rail, feeling the wind while I held him around the waist.

"This's the tough part," Bill said. "Boats get in accidents here; lotta rocks."

"Don't tell her that," Nick said with a between-us-guys chuckle.

"Mostly bad days, though, not like today."

Beyond this Scylla and Charybdis, the shore line disappeared.

"Should be all right here," Bill said, stopping the motor.

He prepared a line for Alex, teaching him and Nick how to do it themselves. I didn't pay attention. My eyes stayed fixed on Alex who leaned over the rail to throw the line further.

The boat rose slightly.

"What's that?" I asked.

"A whale – swimming under us."

"A whale?!" Alex cried, thrilled, and bent down over the rail to see it. "Mamma, there's a whale under us!"

"Yes, darling, I know."

"Daddy, a whale swam under us!"

"I know!" Nick returned, equally delighted.

"Have you ever heard of a whale overturning a boat?" I asked Bill, casual as ever.

"One time; that's all. Nine times out of ten, they're more afraid of you than you are of them."

"Yeah, that's what they said about bears, too. Only we saw a bear and he wasn't afraid of anything. We couldn't get rid of him."

"Must've been a campsite bear. They're not scared of people 'cause the tourists feed 'em."

Ah. Why had no one mentioned "campsite bears" before?

"I got one!" Alex cried.

Bill dropped his line to seize upon the teachable moment.

"Pull up like I showed you. That's it! Keep turning... You got it! Wow, nice one. 'T's a salmon."

The fish flopped onto the floor and flapped around pathetically, staring at death until Bill hit it on the head with a hammer.

Looking like Hemingway's dissolute brother, he placed the fish on the scale.

"Six pounds, two ounces."

"I think I got one," Nick said.

Another triumphant day. Nick and Alex caught a salmon each and after I gave Alex my turn with the fishing rod, he caught an eight pound cod.

Back on shore, we found a picnic area and cooked the day's catch. It remains the only time in Alex' life that he has voluntarily eaten fish.

A minor snafu appeared, however, when it came time to dispose of our garbage: Like Yale University's Skull and Bones building, the bin had no way in.

A fellow picnicker saved the day.

"Got to keep the bears out," he explained, manipulating the top.

"I thought the bears were in the mountains," I replied.

"Got 'em here, too. They go in the garbage, knock everything over. Like big rats."

We had seen a bear and come within a hundred feet of a family of whales. Our boat had been lifted by a whale and for a moment, carried on its back. Alex had caught two fish and proudly eaten them. Nick started to take it easy. The next day, he decided, we would rent a boat to sightsee around the bay on our own, looking for seals sunning themselves on the rocks, or beaver or eagles.

All the motor-boats had been taken so we got a rowboat. Beneath the seat lay a life-vest that fit Alex properly. Also, staying within the bay, we wouldn't lose sight of shore. A tame outing. Bliss.

We rowed around, inspecting the shoreline for wildlife but not finding any. The only action was that of the small whale-watching boats – the kind we'd seen on the cover of the brochure at breakfast the day before – racing past, their red-suited crews splashed and excited, on their way out to sea.

Giving up on wildlife this side of the bay, we were rowing across to the other side when quiet fell and with it, the stillness of foreboding. A passing whale-watching boat had stopped, its passengers uncharacteristically somber. They were watching something right here, now. They seemed to be watching us.

Well, not quite. Nick started as though jolted awake, his eyes widening as he stared straight ahead. I followed his gaze to a puff of something like smoke exploding at the water's surface. We were thirty feet from a whale.

"Let's go," I said tersely.

"They're very gentle," said Nick and rowed closer.

This was no time to impart what I'd learned about the gentleness of whales. But the whale had other plans anyway. Realizing his wrong turn, he puffed away towards the exit of the bay.

Two days later we flew back to New York. It was an uncompromising July day: The sky, the yellow-grey of wet cement; the traffic, choked; the air, unsatisfactory. But I, who do not pray easily, gave prayers of thanks for our safe arrival home.

June 14

"There he goes," said Gretchen. "That's 'The Man Who Can't Get Started.'"

We were in the playground, looking out at the street where one or two people were walking home.

The man Gretchen was talking about, a grizzled geezer in an oversized raincoat, tried to step onto the curb, retreated, tried again. Eventually he succeeded and shuffled up the street.

"Watch – he's going to turn around and go back."

As though in an instructional video which Gretchen was narrating, he did as she described, returning to the curb. Once more he attempted to mount it several times before succeeding. This time he made it further up the street before returning to the curb a third time.

"I thought he had a neurological disorder but Emily says no, he's obsessive-compulsive."

He was like the frog in the math problem who jumps up two feet but falls back one. I assumed that once the man-who-couldn't-get-started arrived home, he didn't go back to the curb.

"I thought he must be on disability but Emily says he works full time."

"What does he do?"

Gretchen looked at me with wonder at the irony of life.

"He works for the I.R.S."

June 18

Julie reports that the day after Mother's Day, her mother-in-law drew her into a corner.

"Did I do something to offend you?" she began. "Because if so, you must tell me…"

Julie didn't know what she was talking about. When her mother-in-law left, she said during the final embrace, "I hope we're friends again."

Now Julie is afraid to call her which will only compound the original misunderstanding.

June 22

A woman just asked nervously, "Are you allowed to smoke in the park?" She seemed afraid someone would tell her Sorry, she'd have to step off the planet.

Update June, 2012: What seemed preposterous twenty years ago has come to pass. A sign at the entrance to the park reads, "No Smoking in Park."

June 23

Tricia's husband, Frank, is an airplane mechanic. He hasn't worked in a year because of a back injury. Tricia has talked of one particular "plane" her husband can't get up.

His Disability has run out and Tricia has gone back to work. Frank stays home and plays Nintendo with their son. Last week, Frank took an aptitude test with the State Department of Labor. He was found to have an aptitude for being a beekeeper, a bookkeeper, a housekeeper and President.

July 2

The park is brushed in tones of swamp and hippo; the bench is slick with rain. Megan is planning tonight's dinner. For her, meals are a celebration and she plans them with as much care. As a fifties mother combed cookbooks for stews, Megan, a nineties mother, hunts for recipes that feature tofu, miso and ginger. She is fulfilled in her three children and would have four more.

"They mark time for us," she says.

July 6

For several days a squirrel has been casing the house. This morning, he squeezed through the window into the kitchen. I didn't think he'd have the nerve; he seemed to understand about animal/human boundaries. But a nearby crackle jolted me out of this delusion. Above the box of Golden Crisp curled a bushy tail. I screamed. He took the hint, bounding back towards the window and home.

July 8

This afternoon's benchmate was a woman with tangerine lipstick and a dress the color of a ripe mango. Her black hair was oiled, an effective advertisement for the hair salon she ran whose card she gave me. I commented on the agility on the monkey bars of her nine-year-old son.

"They said I was going to lose him," she said. "He was 1lb. 13oz. at Q. General Hospital. He had tubes going in him, open heart surgery. I wasn't allowed to hold him so I just stayed there by the incubator praying and singing to him. I already lost one baby so I wasn't going to lose him. They sent a psychologist over 'cause they didn't understand why I wasn't scared the way they were. The psychologist said, 'Do you understand the severity of your son's condition?' I said yes but he's going to make it. The third week he got a tumor in his testicle. I said, 'What is *that*?' We were in there altogether four months but now he's fine."

"Does he have to restrict his activity?"

"No, he can do anything he wants."

She said she'd been sent to talk to me by God. I didn't start going to church as a result of the conversation but I haven't forgotten it either.

July 9

Overheard: "My boyfriend came over and made French toast. Then he put butter and syrup on it as though it was pancakes. Then he spat on it. Then he ate it. I said, 'Wha'd you do that for, you project-grown mother-fucker?'"

July 10

Yesterday a middle-aged woman pushed an old woman in a wheel-chair over to the bench. At the sight of a new companion, the old woman's eyes lit up and she slowly lifted her hand.

"Does she want to shake hands?" I asked the younger woman, who must have been the older one's nurse or daughter.

"Yes," she replied with a Russian accent, "it's

something she remembers how to do it."

I shook the old woman's hand and let it go. A moment later she lifted her hand again with the same expression of pleasure. We shook hands again. A few moments after that we played the scene a third time. Was she remembering her previous pleasure at shaking hands? Or forgetting every ten seconds? Her nurse/daughter covered the hand with the old woman's shawl. The hand fought with the shawl in slow motion, eventually emerging and rising once more. The nurse/daughter covered it more securely. The old woman cried. She didn't speak but we had some heavy eye contact, like characters in a silent movie.

July 13

Inevitably, relationships spark up in the park. Although participants get self-conscious about double entendres: ("Do you come on weekends? Here, I mean, to the park?")

I've never known one of these relationships to go past the flirtation stage. But it does make the daily jaunt, which can be eight hours long, more titillating. ("Will he be there?" Or, when a child the right size comes running down the street, "Is that Peter [his son]?")

Most of my friendships for the last seven years have arisen out of Alex's and some of them have stuck even after the children grew apart. Thus it was in the park that I met Brian, a retired English professor of sixty on his second family. For a long time we'd seen each other but until our children played baseball together, we didn't speak. When we finally did, it was for two hours.

He said that when he first saw me, he thought I was an Au Pair. (He meant this as a compliment.) Later he elaborated on the fantasy: I was from France and lonely because I didn't speak English well. When he saw me writing, he imagined it was to my boyfriend.

As the summer wore on, he talked about his marriage which stayed together mostly for Peter. My antennae shot up but I said nothing. He must have thought I hadn't gotten the point because the next time we met, he repeated the confidence. This time I was ready.

"These two electrons," I said, indicating our children who were, appropriately, running around randomly – "bind us together but they're also the force that keeps us apart." He acknowledged this and anyway, by fall there were other forces keeping us apart.

September 26

"Do you know Tamara Lisko?" Brian asked.

"No."

"You met her a few weeks ago at a roller-blading party."

I remembered – a genial woman. Encounters like that one are what make kids' events endurable for their parents.

"She says you're obsessed with me."

My mind bounced around like a squash ball. For the rest of the day I tried to remember our conversation to figure out how she'd come to this conclusion. We had talked for a few minutes about Brian because he was the only person we both knew, besides the hosts of the party and to talk about them would have been rude. Then I remembered: We had discussed Brian's memoir which had impressed me though not her when she had read an earlier version. She must have been left even colder than she let on because she seems to have thought that anyone who had liked it had lost objectivity, if not their mind.

October 9

Overheard in front of an office building on the way to the park:

"The pudgy one..." (In an exasperated whine)
"Noooo... not him!.. The fat bastard on the fourth floor."

October 25

This afternoon we braced ourselves against the wind and headed for the park. Others had stayed in, however, and Alex became so disheartened by the sight of the empty playground that I offered him a palm-reading at the gypsy's.

Letting us in, a slim, young Arab slipped behind a threadbare curtain from behind which, a moment later, the gypsy appeared. In a long, garish skirt concealing a body that seemed to have been fashioned out of balloons, she looked authentic enough.

Sizing up the situation in true psychic form she said, "It's against the law to read the palm of anyone under sixteen; eighteen for a phone consultation."

I turned to Alex: "Would you like her to read my palm instead?"

"Yes." He nodded with the certainty that befits a young man whose opinion has been consulted.

The gypsy studied my hand briefly. Then, looking into my eyes, she spoke as though reading from a teleprompter.

"I see a long life between eighty-eight and ninety-two years. Are you working or looking?"

(*Aren't you supposed to know?*) "Looking."

"I see paper and pencils."

A safe enough guess; after all, what were the alternatives? Gun and police car? Can of exterminating fluid? "A successful career with much happiness."

"She already has happiness," Alex offered. "She has me."

"You have been disappointed in love but I see a change in the next three years – maybe not marriage but commitment. One of your friends is two-faced and by the end of May, you will know who it is."

I smiled throughout this monologue, more from bemusement than happiness. If she had said she saw an early death, though, I would have been troubled. Do they ever say that?

We reported her predictions to Nick who was saddened about my disappointment in love and pending "commitment." To reassure him would only have been to dwell on it and drive the stake further in. Wishing I'd remembered in time how cheered he had become at a

231

Chinese fortune cookie that promised an imminent change in career at a time when he was contemplating one, with gold to follow, I fluttered on to something else.

Addendum: Many Mays have come and gone since this encounter, without any sign of the two-faced friend. In May of '96, my husband announced he wanted a divorce in order to marry a woman I considered a friend. But I do not think her two-faced. Both she and my husband told their spouses immediately and the commitment was supposed to be mine, not his.

October 29
     "I'm gonna ki' ya, mother fucker... I'm gonna ki' ya..."
     The voice in the street sounded injured rather than threatening. Surely a sizeable percent of violence, at least on the individual level, is the result of a failure of articulation.

November 13
     Overheard at the traffic light while standing behind two old women in printed pants and blouses that hung too loose on their bony frames:

     "You know, where your intestines get tangled up."
     (*Scandalized*) "Are you born with it?"
     "No, no, no. It develops. The intestines go —" (She tangles up her hands.)
     "Oh... And that was a gourmet dish? What was the

other dish they had?"

April 22

Red kite, dipping and sailing, yellow balloon vanishing into blue sky. White ball joins them for a moment, making an illustration for a children's primer.

Alex, Rob and Eduardo are playing basketball, using garbage cans for baskets.

Someone comes out of the men's room shouting, "There's a gun in there!"

It takes a few seconds for everyone to clear out of the park. Everyone, that is, except for Pavel and his grandmother. The problem is not linguistic although Pavel's grandmother doesn't speak English; Pavel is explaining the situation to her in Polish. But Pavel's grandmother escaped the Nazis twice and a gun doesn't faze her.

June 17

Already the trees are grey-brown with the defeated look of New York parks in July. Babysitters sag on the benches. Those on foot drag.

Wendy's mother is nervous. Wendy's father is about to take Wendy for a week. Last year, Wendy's father was released from prison after serving eight years for aggravated assault. He had also threatened Wendy's mother; he said later, to show her what it felt like. The custody arrangements are harsh on Wendy's father. He is allowed to see Wendy for only one week a year. It is that week which is approaching. Last year, when Wendy's father took Wendy for the week, Wendy's mother received a postcard from France. She thinks that was a warning.

August 2

She moves as though trying out a thoughtful style. Whenever I look at her, I find she is already looking at me. She is the pariah of the playground; I wasn't surprised when she said that in high school, she'd been the nerd. A babysitter once observed, "That woman is so nosy." We treat her as some societies treat the police: We are always wondering, "What do you want to know for?" For she does want to know things: Our incomes, rent, weight. As soon as we tell her, she jumps in with advice: We should go for a higher academic degree; own, not rent; join her health club. It is as though we've unwittingly handed her a weapon which she is now using against us.

Today Judith said of her, "Donna was looking for you."

"Why?"

"She's working on a project that involves giving people IQ tests. She wants to do pairs of parents and children."

I thought, *She has become a parody of herself.*

When I ask myself what is so irritating about her, my self answers: She assumes intimacy; if she sees you in a coffee shop, by sitting down at your table. This is behavior I welcome in my friends, of course...

Then there's jealousy – of her easy-going husband;

her accepting mother. But beneath all that is the unpleasant fact that she reminds me of old, and sometimes not so old, parts of myself.

August 8

Since Chris burned down their apartment, they have been living at the S., a welfare hotel. Chris had knocked over a candle in his room and the apartment was uninsured. It is probably not that simple as Chris is always in trouble. Both he and his brother Huey are in Special Ed. although "their gross motor are fine."

My conversation with their mother was interrupted by Alex.

"Huey hit me in the chest," he complained.

"Huey!" reprimanded Huey's mother. "Apologize or I'll leave you with your father."

"Sorry!" shouted Huey and ran back to the game.

"That's an interesting threat," I observed.

"It's a good threat," asserted Huey's mother. "His father hit him in the face with a belt once. I have an Order of Protection saying he can't touch them." (This cast a shadow over the threat but I let it go.)

"How long is it good for?"

"A month, 'til they find him guilty." She smiled disconcertingly, considering the subject matter.

"Were they hurt in the fire?" I asked, returning to our earlier conversation.

"Chris was in the hospital for four hours. I was in for twenty-three. A security guard shimmied down a rope to the terrace, picked him up and swung to another terrace across from ours. Chris was ready to jump, he was so scared."

"What floor was the apartment?"

"Eight. I did all the things Frank Fields says to do on T.V. I felt the doorknob to see if it was cool. Then I went down the stairs. I was given VIP treatment at the hospital. My mother's a clinician. That's above the head nurses. My sister's a nurse and my brother-in-law's a technician. We're getting our equity in the apartment back. If we went back, they'd evict us. The lawyer thinks I'm an idiot. He doesn't realize he's dealing with a college graduate."

"What did you major in?"

"Communication, T.V. production, audio, sound effects."

"Did you work in your field?"

"I was a disc jockey for a year in New Jersey." She put on her disc jockey voice: "WXXX, 85.8 on your A.M. dial."

September 6

The mouse scurried along the wall, looking meek, apologetic, though not so quiet as the simile would have it. I had nothing against him personally but for a marked prejudice against his species.

His companion bolted across the carpet, which aroused less sympathy. Gone were any "cowerin', timorin' beasty" sentiments and loud were the cries of, "Get out of here, you motherfucker."

September 14

Gail has the spacey look of an ex- or possibly still active pot-head. If her expression weren't so vacant, she would be beautiful. But she rarely evinces the least enthusiasm or, for that matter, annoyance. Her most characteristic communication is a shrug.

Her mother died when she was eight, she revealed one day. For the next ten years, her father told her she was stupid. She came to believe it and even now, after a decade of therapy from a woman who did not charge her until she found a job, is acting the part; or maybe her apparent apathy to everything is left over from her junky period.

She reminds me of Caroline, a girl in junior high school in England who couldn't do math. When Miss Ridgefield called on her, Caroline would wag her index finger up and down as though there was a puppet on it and it was the puppet who was speaking. Then she would drawl in a North country accent, "Ah doon't knoo," and Miss Ridgefield would tear at her clown locks that didn't suit her neurotic disposition. We, Caroline's classmates, grew exasperated at these daily scenes, not learning until years later that Caroline was being raised by her older sister, her mother spending those years in a sanatorium.

Gail married a man who smoked even more pot than she did, got a degree in Business Administration while her husband dropped out, then became the family breadwinner while her husband temped.

Now she has separated from him, she says.

How are the kids taking it?

She shrugs: "They haven't noticed."

A few months later, she announces she has found a boyfriend. He also calls her stupid so she has started to read the newspaper. For a while, it is Born Yesterday; she gets angry at what she reads. Then the anger turns on her boyfriend, they break up and the newspaper goes unread once more. The vacant stare comes over her again like cloud-cover.

October 3

We're at the Youth Olympics; Alex, manic with excitement.

"I can't climb with this on." He whips off his jacket. "Let's see, I'll turn my hat backwards." He runs off to scale a thirty foot wall. I find a table in the shade next to a Honduran woman who is studying a paper in English about existential psychology.

October 6

Alex, who has never met a dog he didn't like (although he was subdued for a few days after getting bitten by Hubert, the poodle downstairs who'd been expelled from obedience school) is petting a panting golden retriever whose owner is explaining that dogs sweat through their tongues. This golden retriever is a therapy dog. She goes to nursing homes where she is a soothing presence to bedridden patients and stroke victims. People in these circumstances often don't want other people to see them. But according to this woman, it's been shown that petting dogs can lower blood pressure and alleviate depression. The patients are receptive because they don't feel the dogs are judging them.

The woman is upbeat about these findings but I am disheartened: That we trust each other so little, and rightly so. When I've imagined being in the hospital, there's no one I'd want to see except Alex who is a child and therefore not sizing me up. Everyone else would be making the pilgrimage out of a sense of duty.

(No date) The eclipse approaches steadily, stealing light and turning it a mean, steely sheen, as though portending nuclear disaster. The sky looms low and hard. Since we have been warned not to look, it lures us like Euridice. Afterwards, one of the fathers says that the sunlight on the leaves was itself eclipsed by half-moon shadows.

October 12

A man with no eyes taps his way through the subway car with a stick. He is holding a paper cup.

"Oh, you don't rob banks," he sings, and I wonder if, in addition to being blind, he is mad. "You don't rob banks if you beg."

No, he is not mad.

He is followed by a woman who is more humble than the usual beggars as she addresses the car almost inaudibly:

"Good evening, ladies and gentlemen. Please forgive me for this intrusion. I'm sure you're tired and just want to get home."

She delivers her spiel in a monotone while looking at the floor, as though her script has called on her to play the scene "downcast." Every line trails off in melancholy.

She is a skinny woman who perhaps in earlier life was a dancer. Besides her petiteness, her most noteworthy feature is a green towel tied around her waist. The twist to her presentation is that she needs money for "feminine toiletries." (Hence the towel.) She "humbly begs" us not to mock her for this need. But she is so slight that perhaps this need is a fantasy, amenorrhea being the more likely problem.

Whatever the truth, her pitch works: Somebody fishes out a quarter.

Then a young man drops a few light coins into her box.

"Tell me something," he says. "How come you don't have a job?"

He smiles at the friend next to him and sits back for the show. He is wearing a T-shirt from a University known for its business school.

"Well, Sir," adlibs the woman in her singsong, "I've had a hard time finding a job."

The man has been waiting for this.

"I have a friend who might have a job for you," he says. His sidekick snickers at his wit.

"Well, Sir, I would be interested in talking to your friend," the woman responds in her sing-song. Her gaze, however, remains fixed on the ground.

"Great," says the man. "Why don't you give me

your phone number?"

"Leave her alone," another passenger interjects.

"Yeah," "Let her go do what she has to do," others pitch in.

But the woman is able to defend herself better than we can. In the same forlorn monotone she counters, "I don't have a phone, sir. Would you take a beeper number?"

The man falls for it. "What are you doing with a beeper?"

"Well, Sir," says the woman, "you were sarcastic so I'm being sarcastic also."

Her stance does not change but the words are no longer so humble.

The man rises, followed by his friend.

"I'm sorry if I bothered you," he says as they get off the train.

November 2

I was heading home with two gallons of milk when a man approached calling through a bullhorn, "Geraldine Ferraro! Vote for Geraldine Ferraro in November! See Geraldine Ferraro on Pierrepont Street in two minutes." I hung around.

The candidate appeared, wearing her signature androgynous haircut as well as a gleaming, toothpaste commercial smile which she aimed in all directions. In addition to the herald with the bullhorn, she was surrounded by half a dozen other guys in suits.

"Shake her hand," one of them coaxed a huddle of

pedestrians, as though they were children. And like well brought up children, they offered their hands, having their pictures taken in the process. It was surprising how many people were walking around on a Saturday morning with cameras. (This was before the age of ubiquitous video-cellphones.)

The candidate went into the 99 Cent store followed by Waldenbooks. Only three people were in there but no matter; the point was the photo-op. Then she hit the sidewalk café, Keyfood and finally, the playground.

"Attention, all toddlers!" called her spokesman. "Vote for Geraldine Ferraro on Tuesday."

Not for a moment did the smile falter. Was anyone fooled? Do people vote on the basis of a smile or a handshake? Market research must indicate they do.

"Why aren't any of you wearing dark glasses?" I asked one of her security detail.

"You're several decades behind the times," he replied.

What do they use now, dark contact lenses?

November 18

"Thank God you have your sight," says a blind woman who has asked for help getting to a church on First and Bergen.

"I do. How long have you been blind?"

"I started going blind when I was two. I saw my last baby in 1964. I can see light, shadows, cars. I can see you but I can't tell if you're a man or a woman."

We find the church she is looking for where my role as escort is taken over by a man who is wearing glasses half an inch thick.

November 29

We are watching a documentary about a movie director who, as a child, loved art. To underscore this affinity, which is said to have influenced his adult work, the movie returns several times to a shot of the hand from the Sistine Chapel reaching out to the left side of the screen.

"Why do they keep showing that hand?" Alex asks.

"Maybe to point out the direction the little boy's life later took."

"Backwards?!"

December 5

From a conversation with an ex-army brat who grew up in Third World countries:

"I learned to suck the butts off of honey ants. For Christmas one year I got a piece of coal."

"How horrible."

"No, I deserved it – I drove our car through the living-room. For my 15th birthday, I got a box of ears."

"He boxed your ears?"

"No, we lived in Cambodia. My father gave me a box of ears."

December 8

A conversation with my cousin:

"Dubboo yubboo spubbeak Ubbubby Dubbubby?"

"What?"

"Do you speak Ubby Dubby?"

"No."

"Oh."

"What is it?"

"You just take the syllable 'ub' and put it after the first consonant or group of consonants in each syllable."

"Is that what they speak in Abu Dhabi?"

"I don't know. Tracy Kendall taught it to me. She knows all those phoney languages."

"And now she teaches sign language."

"Right. She can do that in Ubby Dubby as well."

Humor is the result of flawless logic leading to absurdity.

December 13

8th Avenue. A young man, catatonic, frozen in profile like Rodin's Thinker, with his bike cap on backwards. A sign in front of him reads, "I move for money. $1 minimum."

Somebody drops a dollar in the cup. He begins to move as though through molasses.

"I'll move slowly if you give *me* money," another man calls out from the crowd. Is he part of the act? But the human mannequin breaks out of character.

"What' you doing, man?" he accuses and as the argument heats up, the crowd disperses.

December 22

Outside the library, a man proclaims that he has proved the existence of God. The proof is contained in a newspaper he's selling in which he's also offering a reward to anyone who can refute it. Eminent scientists, he maintains, have tried and failed.

I buy the paper. The proof consists of the usual symmetries in the universe which, according to the man, can be no coincidence but must point to a higher power. What is of more interest are the blustering, sarcastic letters of the professors who, if not themselves the product of fabrication, have been baited by the prospect of a reward to attempt to reason with a madman.

October 29

Ahead of the bus as it waits for the light to change is a man on a motorcycle wearing a sweatshirt that bears the logo, "B.I.D."

"Mall security," says the bus driver to a friend in the first seat.

"What does B.I.D. mean?" asks the friend.

"Bring 'em In Dead."

November 4

A few days ago, Henry bought a jade green jacket.

Last night, a muscle-bound man with a purple feather in his hat got out of a large car, held out his hand and said, "Gimme five, man. I like your threads."

This morning Henry gave the jacket away.

November 7

A rich man is speaking to a colleague. "My daughter's interested in banking."

So...? You picked up the phone and had one of your friends give her a job?

Instead the man goes on, "So I bought her a bank in Arizona."

November 22

A ventriloquist is talking to his dummy who, in finest dummy tradition, gives smart-alecky answers.

When the crowd disperses, the ventriloquist takes the dummy off his lap like a tired parent.

He is working his way through Princeton, he says, and makes four hundred dollars a week with his act. Sometimes literary agents throw their cards into his hat along with the change. He's had two book offers.

December 3

Norman Mailer, one of the neighborhood's celebrities, sometimes hangs out at a children's book store whose owner is a friend. When Mailer's book, *Harlot's Ghost,* comes out, it is featured in the store window with the caption, "Illustrated Children's Version."

December 8

Alex' karate school has a new teacher, Sensei Joe. His day-job is teaching remedial reading at a high school in a rough neighborhood. The kids respect him, he says, because they know he's got a black belt. With this under his metaphorical belt, he's free to be friendly with them.

He's also a natural Olympic athlete. When asked where he learned gymnastics he says, "No place. I never took lessons or nothing. I watch the pro's on T.V."

The karate school kids stretch a rope across the room four feet above the ground. Then they clear out of the way to watch Joe perform. He soars over the rope. The kids raise it about three inches. He clears it again. They raise it still more. This time he fails to clear the rope because his head hits the ceiling.

January 15

Avi's father was knifed Thursday night. He survived and is recovering. No one knew what or how much to tell Avi. The problem was obviated when Avi's best friend, Jimmy, told the story the next day in Show and Tell.

March 25

Spring is here. The thaw is on. Everyone's in the park, catching up on the past five months. Tricia ends her account with, "And I had sex!"

"With whom?" Last time we discussed the subject, Tricia hadn't had sex in two years.

"Hector, the guy – remember? – I met at the Laundromat? You know, the funny thing was, I never thought I'd be able to lie. I thought Frank would be able to read it on my face, I'd go all red... Honey, it was so easy."

June 13

The marital problems of Tricia and Frank have escalated. They race around collecting damaging evidence from each other's desk drawers: She's seeing a therapist; he's seeing another woman.

Three Strangers

A middle-aged woman with enormous hair sitting atop her head like cut-out hair on a pudgy, defiant doll. This woman's aggression had found an outlet through her hair.

A woman whose pathology lay in her make-up which was that of Cleopatra on the stage of La Scala. Her hair was dyed jet-black, her eye area sharply defined in a ferocious, Aztec blue. But at the health food store, she spoke to the cashier in the matter-of-fact tones of a born and bred New Yorker. What could have been the deformity that she went to such lengths to hide?

He was leaning on a cane which memory insists on showing as crude, crooked. Upright, he might have been eight feet tall but he was too weak to stand upright. A van waited for him at the curb with two paramedics to help him in.

Five years later, I saw his photograph at an exhibition by Diane Arbus. He was standing next to his normal sized – no, his positively small – parents who were beaming.

Part Four:
Last Act of the Pre-9/11 Era

Aggression

As a young child, she was shy; at eight, bold. As an adolescent, shy again although this time the shyness was a pose. After college, she was so grateful to be done with school that at the supermarket, she let people cut in front of her on line. Once she found a job and was obliged to work only for a paycheck rather than a blessing or condemnation of her soul, her confidence bloomed. She asserted her rights on supermarket lines and encouraged her child to speak his mind.

A spate of killings took place of people who had asserted their rights and spoken their minds. She explained to her child the ways in which the world had changed. He forgot or was overcome with anger and spoke his mind to an eleven-year-old with a knife. She took him home. The next time someone cut in front of her on line at the supermarket, she submitted once more. The man had been joking and restored to her her place. She did not know how to drive and was afraid that if she learned, she would assert her rights with the wrong drivers.

For there were unruly rebels in her mind which she suppressed not out of hypocrisy so much as prudence. Alone, with only the walls as witness, she indulged fantasies of mayhem.

She has observed that the personality of the old is often the negative of the earlier personality. Sweet people reveal mean thoughts; criminals, regret. Go-getters relax; ne'er-do-wells learn Russian. She envisions herself an old woman, her cortex deteriorating. The rebels take over or at least have their say. She becomes the portrait of Dorian Gray, her true self emerging in the pentimento effect of aging. The truths she exposes are hideous for beyond that lies tragedy. Revealed as revolting, she is reviled.

If this happens and she manages to avoid getting shot, she will at least disillusion those who had been taken in by her earlier, gentle philosophy.

Death

When I was five, a family friend, Helen, gave me a life-sized doll for Christmas. From having seen an identical one at Kiddie Korner, I knew that the doll had cost thirty dollars. Helen was not well off. Three years later, she killed herself. We learned that at the age of nine, she had become a prostitute to buy coal for her family. I did not connect this to the extravagant gift or to her suicide.

When I was seven, Great Aunt Dorrie died. I cried for half an hour and never missed her again. Four years later, my mother told me softly that Agnes, a family friend to whom I was close, had died at the age of thirty-six. It was a quarter to four which in England, in winter, was dusk. I retreated to my room without turning on the light and waited for grief. It didn't come. Half an hour later I emerged, thinking I had unwittingly grown up.

In eighth grade, on the day before Easter vacation, we were sitting on our desks waiting for the dismissal bell when Andrew said, "My mother's stage four. They say she's going to die." He let out a hollow laugh and I thought he was making a joke that I didn't understand. No one answered him and I imagined the others all got the joke which explained their nonchalance. Everyone treated the comment as a glitch in the conversation – to be ignored.

Over the Easter vacation, Andrew's mother died. The first day back at school, Andrew was thinner but he behaved the same as before: Cool, indifferent, looking outwards towards the swim-meet and tennis camp.

We had learned of Andrew's tragedy via a phone relay and, awed by the magnitude of the loss, said nothing to Andrew. (At the twenty-fifth reunion, a classmate who'd become a psychologist wondered why we hadn't been told officially about such events and encouraged to attend the funeral.) Andrew himself reported to us with another grim laugh that the Math teacher had patted him on the back and said, "But now you must go on." Andrew must have reached the same conclusion on his own because go on he did and, in defiance of fate, won the swim-meet as well as a silver medal at tennis camp.

Years later, I wondered if he'd been trying to prove his invincibility. When he was a sophomore in college, a male classmate developed a crush on him. Although Andrew had long since come out as gay and enjoyed the popularity afforded a sculpted young athlete, he wasn't interested in this worshipper. Over the summer vacation, the lovesick fan visited him from Texas, paying for the trip by selling his blood along the way. When he arrived, Andrew wrote out a check for his ticket back.

A few months after the death of Andrew's mother, Wendy Krug went home for lunch one day and didn't return for two weeks. Somehow, we learned that her father had died. Since Wendy was a quiet girl whom no one knew well and since her father was the second parent to die that year, there was even less sympathy shown to her. The Math teacher muted his impatience with Wendy for a week before reverting to form.

As this school was predominantly WASP and as my

first school had been predominantly Jewish, I conceived the notion that while Jewish parents divorced, WASP parents died; this, despite my awareness that we were five years older now and so were our parents. (There may have been something to the death-over-divorce ethos though: Over the course of the next five years, two of the fathers in the second school, both married at the time, died in car accidents determined to have been suicides.)

When I was twenty, my own father got headaches and my mother said he had an inoperable brain tumor. I went to the supermarket that afternoon with a newly-acquired understanding of why people at funerals walk slowly; it felt as though I were pushing the cart under water.

That night, my mother and I slept in the same room – except that we didn't sleep. Against the black backdrop of hypnagogia appeared the image of a firebird covered in spangles with shiny scales. He came from what I later described to a friend as "aeons of agony." The fear of seeing him again kept me awake for hours.

The next day, fueled by a nervous energy, I chirped to my mother, "It's funny; I feel O.K. Things seem so normal."

"Oh my darling," sighed my mother, "then why can't we sleep?"

That evening, after Advanced Harmony, I told Professor Louise Talma about my father's diagnosis. We took a walk in the park.

"These are the linden trees that Schubert wrote about

so beautifully," L.T. said as we strolled along the path from 72nd Street. And when a pigeon took off, "Look at that flight!"

We passed the playground at 70th.

"I wonder if the kids really enjoy that stuff," she said. As a child of eight, she'd taken over her late father's role of accompanist for her mother, a singer. It was clear from her attitude now that she thought play a waste of time and had rarely, if ever, gone to a playground herself.

"What time do you eat your evening meal?" she asked, a cue that she wanted to leave. She walked me home, later saying she'd been afraid I might faint.

While my father lay dying, his hospital room became a social hub. Friends from decades before, now divorced, lonely and seeking comfort themselves, were all too willing to offer it.

I dealt with my father's illness calmly, feeling sad but also liberated: Something bad was happening that wasn't my fault! The hardest thing to handle was kindness. I'd learned that fate was indifferent and had developed a reciprocal callousness. What to do when someone broke through that wall to ask with concern about my father? But such moments were rare. Family friends were either oblivious to the seriousness of his condition or discreetly pretending to be.

One night, I came home from the hospital and took a shower. A torrent of sewage issued forth, or so it seemed; it was undoubtedly rust. Finally, I cried.

After my father died, Tanya, a family friend, went

on a buying spree for my younger brother. It was a lesson in materialism: Lose a father; gain an eye-popping bike. Tanya herself went without a winter coat that year. Years later, she was diagnosed with pancreatic cancer and underwent a Whipple procedure which, it was said, involved dozens of blood transfusions. I visited her in the hospital; she asked what I was doing in the neighborhood. I said I'd come to see her. She said that was nice.

She was a beautiful woman who used to change hair color the way she changed locales: Red, white, black; London, New York, Los Angeles. On the occasion of the hospital visit, she looked like a beautiful woman who was sick. During one of the blood transfusions, she acquired AIDS. Two weeks before she died, she called and said that when I had visited her in the hospital, she could tell I thought she looked like a ghoul. The way she dwelled on the word made her sound like one now. I asked her if she wanted to hang up. She said yes and did. Perhaps she wanted to sever ties with old friends to make the final severance less painful.

Someone said that as people approach forty, they start thinking about death. I waited for this to happen but my fortieth birthday came and went with no such preoccupation. Soon after, however, two cysts appeared and a disc slipped. It seemed that while I hadn't been thinking about advancing age, it had been thinking about me.

These days, I keep tabs on death so as to avoid a sneak attack. I scan the obits, first for the age of the deceased. If it is over sixty, I skip the article. In the "B" list in small print, the age is often omitted but clues like "grandfather of…" "mother-in-law of…" reveal that the dead saw their children to adulthood so that still greater tragedy does not dwell between the lines. When the dead are young, I check to see whether their parents have survived them and am relieved when they have not.

My sister-in-law also checks the age first. Perhaps most people do, which is why the paper often puts it up front in the title or the first paragraph. "I'm always sad when they're young," she says.

More than sadness, I feel an infusion of relief, as though the gods have filled their quota of youth so that according to some divine law of probability, they'll ease off for a while. Of course, a higher number of dead young people could simply mean that the probability of dying young has risen.

In the In Memoriam column, readers address notes to relatives; for instance, on the anniversary of their death. I didn't think I knew anyone gullible enough to do this but a few months ago, a note appeared from one of my more cosmopolitan friends to his deceased ex-wife.

A curiosity of the column is that each year, on August 22, a society with a P.O. Box in New Orleans pays tribute to the memory of Richard Plantaganet, (King Richard III.)

It's a marvel to read how much the dead are missed and what fruitful lives they have led. To focus on the obits would lead one to believe the world a harmonious place that ran smoothly, love greasing its parts.

Three True Stories

Rhonda had a son of six. One day at school, he fell out the window and died. The headmaster of the school told Rhonda. A year later, the two married.

Was this the silver lining to the cloud of tragedy? Or did the Headmaster's proposal stem from guilt in which case, was the marriage his penance? Or, most cynical of all, (particularly for that bygone era,) was he heading off a law-suit?

A respected historian was befriended by a rich old man whose only child, a daughter, was ill and would die young. The old man told the historian, "If you marry my daughter and take care of her until she dies, I will make you my heir."

Both sides kept to the agreement. It was not known how much the daughter knew or suspected of the arrangement.

A mother died leaving three children, ages six, nine and thirteen. After some prodding, the father, an uppercrust Englishman for whom such actions went against the grain, asked them if they wished to see a therapist. Two did. The nine-year-old said she didn't because she saw her mother in her dreams.

The Days Since
(October, 2001)

*Written before the political battles and education which
led to The Moron's Guide to Global Collapse

In Union Square, a shrine appears
and then another 'til the place
attracts reporters who report
its volunteers' hard work and grace.
A fireman with a haunted look
sits on the bench, his eyes rimmed red.
A woman asks him, "Coffee? Bagel?"
Without a word, he shakes his head.
Around, a wall of Wanted posters,
"wanted" in that other sense:
The Missing, all so very young.
The pictures stay up on the fence
for weeks, for who will tear them down?
Who'd commit that sacrilege?
And yet one night, somebody does
when hope takes its last breath. It was,
in retrospect, a far-fetched dream
that anybody would be found
and nursed to health when a million tons
of stuff had crumbled to the ground.

A fire truck, not red but beige
with dust in which someone has written,

260

"God bless the New York Fire Department." Someone else has drawn a heart.
Across the street, the rectory,
where Father Mychal combed his hair,
they said at his memorial,
and raced downtown to die in prayer.

T-shirts needed! Dogfood! Boots!
AOL provides a list,
all obsolete; they're overwhelmed
downtown. The chance is sorely missed
by millions who want to help out
and be part of this aweful thing.
For nothing matters next to this.
God bless America they sing
at services all over town,
at meetings of the PTA,
at school, in concert on TV
they sing from sea to shining sea.

The weeks go on and still the fire burns.
At Fulton Street the smell
still greets whoever's on the train
and says, "Ascend and witness Hell."
Upstairs the crowd stands quietly
and takes it in. The tired cops
sigh, "All right, move it; that's enough,"
to tourists snapping photo ops.
For foreigners are less appalled,

they, never having known it when.
Its metal's bent like willow branches.
The church clock's stopped at five to ten.
W-T-C, those letters,
now a code for grief and fear;
when I was studying music, they
stood for the Well-Tempered Clavier.
A few blocks down, at Trinity,
the ancient graveyard's buried, itself,
in dust. Another wrenching sign:
Its clock is stopped at five to nine.

Home is no relief – indeed
it fuels the burning energy
that drives us to consume more facts;
here life is centered on TV.
The people falling upside down,
A man says he stayed in the room
by clinging to the doorknob which
saved him from the fierce vacuum.
A man and woman holding hands
fall – Lovers? Strangers? Who cares, now? –
willing, finally, to greet
Death just to get out of the heat.
The cast of characters comes on:
Rumsfeld, grim, tightlipped, thank God,
Powell and Fleischer jauntier
as they joust with the press. It's odd
how recent enemies are heroes,

Giuliani, for example
and former wits are reverent
towards our formerly witless President.
No one ridicules him now.
Indeed, he's less ridiculous.
If he said, "Pakistanians" now,
no one would make such a fuss.
He gears us up for what's in store:
This is a whole new kind of war.
The women, Paula Zahn, Queen Noor;
at one A.M. her time, Amanpour
reporting from Islamabad
in khaki, like a Sabra, say.
"She has a son, you know."
"She does? But where is she from, anyway?"
"Eat dinner out! Go spend your money!"
they tell us. "See a play! A game!"
"Don't let the bastards get you down!"
(And don't buy Middle Eastern honey.)
"Be careful of suspicious mail!
Don't touch it, move it; leave the room!
It could contain an anthrax powder!
Call 911!" You can't assume
the world's a friendly place these days.
Despite the work of CIA,
the FBI's half million tips,
we're speeding towards Apocalypse.

New Yorkers soon are introduced

to war and its accoutrements:
Gas masks, filters, body suits,
an unaccustomed vigilance.
We acquire expertise
in germs and chemicals right quick:
Sarin, hemorrhagic virus;
meanwhile, a little Arabic.
A money system based on trust
that leaves no trace, the East's hawala;
schools that feed while they instill
a willingness to die for Allah.
We're not so loved as we had thought.
The world prepares for years of war
as oppressed people rise protesting,
"We won't take it anymore!"
In China, the disaster footage
is seen as just another thriller,
interspersed with scenes from films
found on the shelf, next to Godzilla.
In Pakistan, the angry mob
protests American arrogance.
From Malaysia to Nigeria,
many think we've had our recompense,
especially the Taliban
who escort foreign journalists
to show them what the angry mob'll
avenge: The mile miss outside Kabul.

Monday morning: To the doctor.

After all, life must go on.
"Oh by the way, could I have Cipro?"
The doctor, adamantly con,
however, thinks I am in error
to give in to those guys whose aim
is not just to destroy and kill
but also to instill in us, terror.

The city's quieter, subdued.
Where did everybody go?
Will we be quarantined? Cut off?
Do they know something we don't know?
I walk down to the water's edge.
A child places a bouquet
at a shrine outside the park
where I used to bring my son to play.
A picture rests against the fence
to show the viewer where the World
Trade Center stood before that day
when we all lost our innocence.

Endnotes

1   Rosalyn Tureck
Fearsomely demanding keyboard player dedicated to the music of JS Bach
Jessica Duchen   The Guardian,   18 July 2003
http://www.theguardian.com/news/2003/jul/19/
guardianobituaries.artsobituaries

2   Isaiah Berlin, footnote "He was briefly back in Russia in 1945, doing intelligence work for the British embassy in Moscow (continuing employment he had had in wartime Washington)." http://www.economist.com/node/352783 Sir Isaiah Berlin, an Oxford phenomenon, died on November 5th, aged 88   Nov 13th 1997

3   Rorem, Ned (23 May 1982). "The Composer and the Music Teacher". New York Times. Retrieved 21 February 2012. http://en.wikipedia.org/wiki/User:Pgbrown/Nadia_Boulanger#cite_note-Rorem-66

4   http://en.wikipedia.org/wiki/Root_race

5   Who said, "Let them eat cake?" http://answers.yahoo.com/question/index?qid=1006010603394

6   It was nothing of the kind. Some fascinating studies point out the ways in which the events depicted in the Bible may be seen as metaphors for the movements of the stars. http://www.bethlehemstar.net/starry-dance/the-birth-of-a-king/

7   That interview with "Toby" is now available in five parts on the internet beginning here: http://www.youtube.com/watch?v=_VeLOIxiG4c

8   Riyadh Compound Bombings, Wikipedia http://en.wikipedia.org/wiki/Riyadh_compound_bombings
       Shock And Fear In Riyadh by CBS News State Department Reporter Charles Wolfson http://www.cbsnews.com/2100-18568_162-553938.html

9   "Having earlier worked in Saudi Arabia in a similar capacity, the legal consultant cited the practice followed in the kingdom."
       No law on heat-linked work stoppage Sunil Rao,

Gulf News
       Published: 00:00 August 22, 2002
       http://gulfnews.com/news/gulf/uae/general/no-law-on-heat-linked-work-stoppage-1.396920

10   When this article appeared in Counterpunch, I received two angry emails correctly pointing out the origin of this criterion in the Koran's code on cleanliness.

11   Changing patterns of hepatitis A prevalence within the Saudi population over the last 18 years by Faleh Al Faleh, Suliman Al Shehri, Saleh Al Ansari, Mohammed Al Jeffri, Yaqoub Al Mazrou, Ahmad Shaffi,
       Ayman A Abdo World J Gastroenterol 2008

December 28; 14(48): 7371-7375; wjg@wjgnet.com World
Journal of Gastroenterology ISSN 1007-9327; doi:10.3748/
wjg.14.7371 © 2008 The WJG Press. All rights reserved.
http://www.wjgnet.com/1007-9327/14/7371.pdf

12   Filipino? Tagalog? Pilipino? TAGALOG LANG
http://tagaloglang.com/The-Philippines/Language/filipino-
tagalog-pilipino.html

About the Author

Jenna Orkin is an author, journalist and co-founder of the World Trade Center Environmental Organization as well as other Lower Manhattan organizations that revealed and testified to the lies of the United States Environmental Protection Agency following 9/11. A graduate of Oxford University and New York Law School as well as a former Teaching Fellow in Music History at Juilliard, she has been in Who's Who in America since 2004 and Who's Who in the World since 2008. Currently she writes and does research for Collapsenet.com.

Other Books by Jenna Orkin

The Moron's Guide to Global Collapse

26164375R00147

Made in the USA
Lexington, KY
20 September 2013